༄༄ བླ་མ་མ་བརྗེད་རྟག་ཏུ་གསོལ་བ་ཐོབ།།

རང་སེམས་མ་ཡེངས་རང་ངོ་རང་གིས་ལྟོས།།

འཆི་བ་མ་བརྗེད་ཆོས་ལ་བསྐུལ་མ་ཐོབ།།

སེམས་ཅན་མ་བརྗེད་སྙིང་རྗེ་བསྔོ་སྨོན་གྱིས།།

_____

Do not forget the Lama
Pray to him at all times.

Do not be carried away by thoughts
Watch the nature of mind.

Do not forget death
Persist in Dharma.

Do not forget sentient beings
With compassion dedicate your merit to them.

THE SPIRIT OF TIBET

The Life and World of Khyentse Rinpoche, Spiritual Teacher

With a remembrance by
HIS HOLINESS THE DALAI LAMA

Excerpts from the writings of
KHYENTSE RINPOCHE AND OTHER TEACHERS

Photographs and narrative by
MATTHIEU RICARD

Translations by
THE PADMAKARA TRANSLATION GROUP
A SHECHEN FOUNDATION PROJECT

APERTURE

APERTURE GRATEFULLY
ACKNOWLEDGES
THE GENEROUS
SUPPORT OF THE
E. T. HARMAX
FOUNDATION.

(endpapers) *Delicate birch trees cover a hillside in Wu Tai Shan, known in Tibetan as Riwo Tse Nga, the five-peaked mountain range in central China that is sacred to Mañjushri.*

(page 2) *Near Derge, in Eastern Tibet, Khyentse Rinpoche crosses the 17,000 foot Gosé-La ("White Hair") Pass, so named because it is said to take so long to climb that by the time you reach the top your hair will have turned white. In 1988 Khyentse Rinpoche traveled the route in a sedan chair carried by local people from villages along the way, all eager to take turns of some fifteen minutes. They walked at such a speed that the rest of his party, even carrying nothing, found it difficult to keep up with them.*

(right) *The valley of Junyong, near the birthplace of Mipham Rinpoche, the great teacher who blessed Khyentse Rinpoche shortly after his birth.*

Contents

AUTHOR'S NOTE

This book is an offering. It is an offering to my teacher, Dilgo Khyentse Rinpoche, to my spiritual companions, and to all those who might rest their eyes for a while on these images.

In 1967, I traveled to Darjeeling in India and met my first teacher, Kyabje Kangyur Rinpoche. I have lived permanently in the Himalayas since 1972. After Kangyur Rinpoche left this world, I spent twelve years with Khyentse Rinpoche in Bhutan, India, and Nepal, studying with him and serving him. During this time, I became a Buddhist monk. I was fortunate enough to accompany Khyentse Rinpoche three times to Tibet.

Over the years, I have taken photographs of my teachers and the world around them. My main aspiration in doing so was to share the incredible beauty, strength, and depth of their world.

According to the Buddhist teachings, the Buddha-nature is present in every living being, and the natural state of the phenomenal world, when not misconstrued under the power of negative thoughts, is perfection. Positive qualities, such as a good heart, are believed to reflect the true and basic fabric of human beings. In photography, my hope is therefore to show the beauty of human nature. Even in intense suffering there can be dignity and beauty; even in the face of destruction and persecution there can be hope. This is particularly true for Tibet and its people, who have succeeded in retaining their joy, inner strength, and confidence even while being subjected to a human and a cultural genocide.

After Khyentse Rinpoche's death in 1991, his grandson and spiritual heir, Shechen Rabjam Rinpoche, with the support of many of his grandfather's disciples, vowed to continue his work and perpetuate his teachings at the Shechen Monasteries in Nepal and Tibet and their branch organizations in other parts of the world. It is under the auspices of the Shechen Foundation that this book has been prepared.

The condensed biography of Khyentse Rinpoche was compiled from his own written autobiography (which covers the early years of his life), some audio recordings in which he recounted certain episodes of his life in Tibet, and interviews with his wife and disciples. We are also very grateful to Erik Pema Kunsang for allowing us to incorporate excerpts from his translation of two oral accounts of Khyentse Rinpoche's life by Tulku Orgyen Topgyal. The poems, songs, and teachings are from a variety of sources, which are detailed on page 152.

The different elements of the text were translated from the Tibetan or written and edited by the Padmakara Translation Group, an international group of translators who have practiced and studied Buddhism for several decades under the guidance of eminent Tibetan masters. This group is devoted to the accurate and literate translation of Buddhist texts and oral teachings into Western languages. Based in Dordogne, France, the Padmakara Translation Group is directed by Pema Wangyal Rinpoche and Jigme Khyentse Rinpoche, and for this book included John Canti, Ani Jimba, Daniel Staffler, Wulstan Fletcher, and myself. Special thanks are due to Jill Heald, Wendy Byrne, and Vivian Kurz for their invaluable contribution to this project.

I am particularly grateful to Henri Cartier-Bresson for his encouragement, inspiration, and support for the goals of this book, and to Michael Hoffman, without whose enthusiasm, wisdom, and experience it could never have matured into a reality. Finally, I am profoundly grateful to His Holiness the Dalai Lama, who has always treated Khyentse Rinpoche's disciples with great kindness, for agreeing to share with us some of his own memories and feelings as a prelude to this book.

M.R.

REMEMBRANCE

Khyentse Rinpoche is one of my most revered teachers. From him I received many important teachings, especially from the Ancient Tradition (*Nyingma*) concerning the experience of awareness, or *rigpa*.

From the first time we met, I had a very good impression of him. Subsequently, I had clear indications, in profound experiences and dreams, that we had some special karmic connections. As a result, I began to receive teachings from him. Today I feel very grateful to him for all the help he has given me.

Khyentse Rinpoche did not start out with a high rank in the religious hierarchy, but became a great teacher by developing complete and authentic accomplishments. As an incarnation of the nineteenth-century Tibetan master Jamyang Khyentse Wangpo, he began even as a child to manifest the spiritual potential he had inherited from former lives. He received teachings from many masters, and instead of just leaving those teachings on the pages of his books, he actually put them into practice and gained direct experience of them.

At quite a young age, he took to the life of a hermit and devoted all his time to contemplating the teachings and experiencing their real meaning. He reached the very essence and vital point of meditational practice, and as a result became a holder of the living tradition—the empowerments, transmissions, and pith-instructions—of the eight principal spiritual lineages that flourished in Tibet and included the traditions of both sutra and tantra.

Besides his other hidden qualities, he was manifestly a great scholar and practitioner. I particularly appreciated his deeply nonsectarian outlook. There existed in Tibet a number of different spiritual traditions, corresponding to different ways of practicing, each characterized by certain unique features: one aspect of the practice may be given more or less emphasis, or some important point of the teachings may be explained in a particular way. If one studies these different traditions, one finds that they complement one another. A nonsectarian approach is therefore very useful for one's own practice, as well as for helping to sustain the Buddhist teachings.

Despite his wide renown and large following, Khyentse Rinpoche always remained very gentle and humble. His deep spiritual experience was obvious, but he was never proud of his knowledge. This is something very remarkable. He was equally kind to all, whether high or low, and it is true to say that he was never heard to say anything that would bring hurt or pain to others.

He worked tirelessly to preserve and spread the Buddha's teachings for the sake of all beings, saving and reproducing rare scriptures that had almost disappeared, restoring monasteries that had been destroyed, and above all teaching. Even in his old age, he was always ready at any time to give textual explanations, empowerments, and pith-instructions to anyone who could become a genuine holder of the lineage. Everything he did was directed solely toward helping others and preserving the teachings. He also wrote a large number of treatises and commentaries.

Khyentse Rinpoche was a model for all other holders of the teachings. We should not only admire his inconceivable knowledge, wisdom, and accomplishment, but, more importantly, we should follow his example and emulate those qualities ourselves. The Buddha's teachings are of enormous value for everyone, not only to dedicated practitioners but to lay people, too, and we must all try our best to practice and implement them, and to emulate the great teachers who have followed him. That is the best way to fulfill our teacher's wishes, the best offering we can make to him. As far as I am concerned, I feel that to offer my spiritual practice and accomplishment to my teacher would be the best way to please him, and I request all my spiritual friends to generate the same aspiration. My belief is that practitioners of the present can benefit greatly from learning about how the great practitioners of the past endeavored on the path.

As Rinpoche's student, I would like to share with his other students my feeling that we are very fortunate to have met him and received his teachings. What we received from him was priceless. Now, therefore, it is essential that we implement his teachings in our daily life, so that we become good students of such a good lama.

Deep spiritual experiences, which seem to transcend logical explanation, are not easily expressed in words or transmitted by means of verbal explanation. They depend, rather, on the inspiration and blessings received from the spiritual lineage through one's teacher. This is why in Buddhism (and particularly Vajrayana Buddhism), the practice of Guru Yoga—"union with the teacher's nature"—is given such great importance. This is all the more so for the realization of awareness, *rigpa*, in the Great Perfection tradition. Since the practice of Guru Yoga is so important, the qualities of the teacher himself are extremely important, too. The qualities necessary for an authentic teacher were described in great detail by the Buddha himself in many sutras and tantras. All of these qualities I found in Khyentse Rinpoche.

When the Buddhist teachings began to flourish in Tibet, the blessings of Guru Padmasambhava, who brought Buddhism to Tibet, were a very important factor. His prayers and his compassion established a very special connection between him and Tibet. We are now living in an age in which, from a spiritual point of view, conditions have deteriorated. People are very intelligent and inventive; but the quality they often lack is true human goodness. Their intelligence is used in more and more destructive ways. The Tibetans themselves have been going through a very difficult period, with the widespread destruction that Tibet and Tibetan Buddhism have suffered. And all over the world, all sorts of upheavals and misfortunes have arisen. At such difficult times, the blessings of Guru Padmasambhava are essential, and I feel that the same is true of Khyentse Rinpoche's blessing, since he had a very special connection with Guru Padmasambhava.

This, then, is about my teacher.

I am very pleased with the publication of *Journey to Enlightenment*, this biography of Khyentse Rinpoche illustrated with beautiful photographs. With my prayers that my teacher's wisdom may permeate our minds, I would like to thank the photographer Ven. Konchok Tenzin (Matthieu Ricard), the publisher, and all those who have collaborated in this work.

The Dalai Lama, March 26, 1996

INTRODUCTION

This book attempts to open a door into a world both ancient and yet remarkably relevant to our times, and to provide a glimpse—from the inside—of a Tibetan Buddhist teacher's life and of a unique culture that, despite the upheavals in its homeland, still survives in all its authenticity.

For more than a thousand years, Buddhist culture flourished in Tibet as the foundation of a whole society. Monks and nuns accounted for up to a quarter of the population, a figure probably unmatched elsewhere in human cultures or history. Spiritual practice was clearly the chief goal in life, and lay people too—men and women, nomads, peasants, and traders—considered that their day-to-day activities, however necessary, were nevertheless of secondary importance compared to this deeper aspiration.

Such universal commitment to Buddhist practice was without doubt fostered by Buddhism's very pragmatic approach to becoming a better human being, through the unraveling of the very experiences of happiness and suffering, and their causes. It must have been nourished, too, by the dramatic beauty, vastness, and pristine purity of Tibet's landscape, which provided an uplifting setting for the contemplative life. Above all, Tibetan Buddhism produced a number of remarkable men and women who, as living examples of enlightenment, were a constant inspiration to the community.

Typically, the journey of someone disillusioned with materialistic or self-centered goals starts with the search for a teacher and the growth of confidence in that teacher and his instructions. The student then studies and meditates with great dedication in monasteries or mountain hermitages or, in the case of householders, at home during the considerable leisure time afforded by Tibet's traditional way of life. Some practitioners in their turn eventually become qualified teachers, capable of contributing to the welfare of others. Indeed, the aim of every disciple as he perfects himself is to gain the means with which others can be truly helped.

The Buddhist path is thus rooted in altruism. On a cultural level, this concern for others is expressed as nonviolence—nonviolence toward other people, toward animals, and toward the environment. Tibetans shunned war, hunting, and fishing, and avoided any degradation of their country and its rich natural resources through overexploitation.

All who travel to the Land of Snows or meet refugees outside Tibet are struck by that unique blend of cheerfulness, fortitude, and deeply ingrained confidence in the Buddhist teachings that characterizes Tibetans.

In the late 1950s, a sudden blast of sorrow tore through a thousand years of peace as Communist China invaded Tibet. In the 1960s came the Cultural Revolution, and during the twenty years that followed, one million Tibetans—a sixth of the population—died of persecution or starvation. Six thousand monasteries and temples were destroyed. Books were burned or thrown into the rivers. Precious bronze images were melted down and cast into cannons and guns. The genocide was both human and cultural.

Over a hundred thousand Tibetans, led by their spiritual and temporal leader, the fourteenth Dalai Lama, fled to India and other neighboring countries, where they kept alive the flame of freedom and the depth and breadth of Tibetan culture. Many great masters of the four main schools of Tibetan Buddhism continued to teach, and founded new monasteries in the lands of their exile.

Following Mao Zedong's death, Tibet underwent a minor degree of liberalization. In 1981, after twenty-five years of complete silence, Tibetan refugees started to receive news from relatives who had stayed in Tibet. Some monasteries were rebuilt, and a limited number of monks were allowed to resume their Buddhist studies and monastic training. A far cry from true freedom, these improvements were nevertheless welcome. A bridge was built between old teachers still alive in Tibet and a younger generation surprisingly eager to study and to join the monasteries. The Chinese realized that decades of persecution had changed nothing of

Tibetan attitudes. The regime has since been turning to other methods. Rather than attempting to reform the Tibetans themselves, they now aim at diluting the Tibetan population with a tide of Chinese colonizers to the point of making Tibetans a minority in their own country. Unless quickly stopped, population transfer may very well succeed where persecution failed, and extinguish from our world a unique people and culture.

At the very center of the Tibetan world is the lama, or spiritual teacher. In 1985, one of the greatest Tibetan lamas of recent times, Dilgo Khyentse Rinpoche, visited Tibet after thirty years in exile. The fervor and strength of the crowds that flocked to meet him may be the clearest sign that in Tibet a renaissance is still possible. At the same time, this is no mere return to the past. Partly as a result of their forced departure into exile, many Tibetan Buddhist teachers have been able to inspire and teach people from all over the world, who have recognized the enormous and universal value of this singular culture.

In this book we portray Khyentse Rinpoche, the archetype of the spiritual teacher, someone whose inner journey led him to an extraordinary depth of knowledge and enabled him to be, for all who met him, a fountain of loving kindness, wisdom, and compassion.

Prayer flags, printed with prayers and sacred images. It is said that wherever the wind that touches them goes, it will carry the beneficial power of the prayers to any beings it meets. The other elements are used similarly: prayers carved in the rocks, big prayer wheels turned by the running water of mountain streams, or smaller ones turned by the heat rising from the flame of a butter lamp.

THE EARLY YEARS

Khyentse Rinpoche was born in 1910 as the fourth son of the Dilgo family, which traced its descent from the great ninth-century king of Tibet, Trisong Detsen. The family home, his birthplace, was in the valley of Denkhok in Kham—the easternmost of Tibet's four main provinces. Kham was made up of many small kingdoms, of which the largest and most influential was Derge. Khyentse Rinpoche's grandfather, Tashi Tsering, and later his father, were both ministers to the king of Derge. In his autobiography, Khyentse Rinpoche recounts:

"One of my ancestors died in battle for the king of Derge. As compensation, the Dilgo family was awarded an estate of rich land in the valley of Denkhok. In my great-grandfather's time, the family used to send a servant couple to Denkhok every spring to work the fields and supervise what happened there, and then return home to Derge for the winter. This servant couple were very fond of one of the many sons in the Dilgo family, my grandfather, Tashi Tsering. He was not what you would call a favorite son. In fact, there were so many sons that he was hardly looked on with any favor at all, so the servant couple had adopted him in all but name.

"One year, it was decided that the two servants should move permanently to Denkhok. The couple tried to keep their departure a secret from Tashi Tsering to spare him the distress of separation, but the boy had already found out. As they were leaving, he dressed himself for the journey and insisted on following them. Finally, the family decided to let him go to live with them in Denkhok.

"As he grew up, he became a very influential man in Derge and an important minister in the Derge government, admired as much for his honesty as for his intelligence and learning. His wife was a devout Buddhist and spent long periods meditating on the Buddha of compassion, Chenrezi. Their son was my father.

Khyentse Rinpoche in his twenties, wearing the thin white robe of his years in retreat (see page 41).

"Our family's principal lamas[1] were Jamyang Khyentse Wangpo and Jamgön Kongtrul. Despite my grandfather's warning that Jamyang Khyentse would certainly disapprove, my father as a young man often used to go hunting. One day the whole family went to Dzongsar Monastery to see Jamyang Khyentse, who called my father to his room and asked, 'Have you not been killing animals?'

"'Yes,' he replied nervously, 'I have killed a few.' It was considered unthinkable to lie to the lama.

"'The Dilgo family is wealthy; there's no need for you to hunt,' said Jamyang Khyentse. 'Today you must vow never to go hunting again.' He took a sacred image and placed it on my father's head. My father felt uncomfortable and ashamed.

"When he returned to their quarters, my grandfather asked him, 'What did Rinpoche say to you?' My father was too upset to answer. 'Did he tell you not to go hunting?' insisted my grandfather.

"'Yes, he did,' my father admitted.

"My grandfather had said nothing about my father's hunting to Jamyang Khyentse, who could only have known about it through his great clairvoyance. From that time onward my father never hunted again.

"My mother was the daughter of another minister in the Derge government. She was always very gentle, while my father's temperament was more strict.

"Our house was as huge as a palace, and had more than a hundred rooms, including several beautiful temples. In the west wing was the main temple, and however loud the musical instruments were played there, they could not even be

[1] The word *lama* means a spiritual teacher. Important lamas, often incarnate ones, are accorded the title *Rinpoche*, meaning "precious one." Many lamas, though by no means all, are monks (i.e., have taken vows of celibacy and follow other rules). Conversely, there are many monks who would not necessarily be considered lamas, even though the use of the word is often extended in everyday speech as a polite form of address for any senior monk.

heard in the east wing where my parents had their quarters. When I was around seven I used to wrap myself in a red shawl like a monk, asking our servants to do the same, and eight or so of us would perform ceremonies together. When my father's many visitors saw us they would ask which monastery we were from, which made me giggle.

"In summer, after some study in the morning, I used to set off up the mountain and pitch a tent in one of the beautiful meadows full of flowers. I would stay there the whole day long and play in the stream. In the late afternoon, around four, I would go back home for more study.

"My family owned over ten thousand animals. Most were herded by nomad families in return for a share of the income they brought. For about two months, in late spring after the snow melted, there was work for many people in our fields, and for another two months at harvest time in autumn.

"When my father was in his fifties our house in Denkhok collapsed in an earthquake, killing both of my grandparents and my eldest brother.

"Shortly before the birth of my parents' third son, the household's resident lama had several auspicious dreams. In one of them he dreamt that a famous pair of cymbals kept at Benchen Monastery were being played in a crowded gathering at our house. He interpreted this to mean that the expected son would be the incarnation of Sangye Nyenpa, a great teacher whose seat was Benchen. But my father was furious, as he had no wish to lose his sons to the monastic system. He told the lama that, had he not lived for so long with the family and been such a good friend, he would give him a hundred strokes of the whip. He also made the lama swear to keep quiet about his dream. However, some time later the patriarch Karmapa issued a proclamation that this child was, indeed, Sangye Nyenpa Rinpoche, and reluctantly my father was obliged to give his son to Benchen Monastery. He worried that any more sons he might have would also be claimed as incarnate lamas.

"While my mother was pregnant with me, her fourth son, the family went to visit Mipham Rinpoche, a great lama who lived in a hermitage about an hour's walk from our estate. Mipham Rinpoche immediately asked if my mother was pregnant. This my parents confirmed, and asked him if it was a boy or a girl.

"'It is a son,' said Mipham Rinpoche, 'and the moment he is born it is important that you let me know.'

"He gave my mother a protection cord and some blessed pills of Mañjushri, the Buddha of wisdom (see page 36), to be given to me at birth. The day I was born, before I had any of my mother's milk, a lama duly wrote on my tongue the seed-syllable *Dhi*,[1] the quintessence of Mañjushri's mantra, using the powdered pills mixed with saffron water.

"When I was three days old my parents took me to see Mipham Rinpoche, who said something to the effect that I was a special child. From birth, I had long black hair that came down over my eyes. My father asked if it should be cut, but

Mipham Rinpoche said no and tied it up himself in five bunches, like Mañjushri's hair. At my mother's request, he gave me a name, Tashi Paljor (auspicious glory), writing it down himself on a slip of paper that my mother afterward always kept in her prayer book.

"A while later, my parents took me to see Mipham Rinpoche again. He blessed me by performing a Mañjushri empowerment ceremony and said, 'Throughout all your future lives, I will take care of you.' I feel that this blessing of his was the single most important event in my life.

"When I was a year old, a great lama of the Sakya lineage, Loter Wangpo, came to our house. He was the foremost Sakya disciple of Jamyang Khyentse Wangpo. At that time there was an epidemic in the area and my parents, afraid that I would catch the disease, arranged for my mother and myself to stay high up on the mountainside with one of our nomad tenants. When Loter Wangpo arrived my mother brought me down to see him.

"He gave me his blessing, chanted some invocations, and said to my mother, 'This is a child different from all others. I want to see the lines on his palms.' He got up—with difficulty, for he was a heavy man—and took me to the door of the temple. Looking at my hands in the daylight he said, 'This is indeed a remarkable child.'

"He took me back to his quarters and gave me a bead from Jamyang Khyentse's rosary, which he wore around his neck in a small pouch of red brocade. He also made a silk protection cord and asked his attendant to bring a long ceremonial scarf of white silk with auspicious wishes woven into it. The attendant, being a bit niggardly, brought an ordinary silk scarf, and Loter Wangpo angrily sent him back to look for a more special one. The attendant returned with an old, stained scarf, and again, even more angrily, Loter Wangpo sent him to get a new, pure white scarf.

"My mother was very modest and kept saying, 'Oh no, that one is fine.'

"But Loter Wangpo said, 'No, I must have an immaculate scarf. This boy is the emanation of my teacher, Jamyang Khyentse Wangpo. For three days in a row I have had dreams and visions of Khyentse Wangpo, and when I saw the boy I had no doubt at all.'

"In any important matter, my father would seek advice from Mipham Rinpoche, and at this time Mipham Rinpoche said, 'It is still a little too early to publicly recognize the boy as Khyentse's incarnation. It might provoke obstacles.'

"So for the time being my father did not offer me to Loter Wangpo, nor was I sent to Dzongsar Monastery.

---

[1] Each Buddha is associated with a particular Sanskrit letter or syllable that is a condensed form of the mantra connected with this Buddha. When visualizing a Buddha, one begins by visualizing such a syllable, which then melts into light and transforms itself into the Buddha—hence the term "seed syllable."

"When I was two years old, Mipham Rinpoche died, and Shechen Gyaltsap Rinpoche came to participate in the funeral ceremonies. During his stay, I visited him regularly. He told my father that I should be brought to him later at Shechen Monastery, as I would be of benefit to the Buddhist teachings and to all beings. My father asked him what indications he had of this. Shechen Gyaltsap Rinpoche, who rarely spoke of such things, replied that the night before he had had a dream in which the image in our temple of Tseringma, the Protectress of Long Life, turned into the goddess herself and told him to take care of this child, who

would be of benefit to the teachings. My father, who was very direct, said that if this was really true he would allow me to go to Shechen. But if it was just for me to occupy a throne at the monastery and get caught up in ecclesiastical politics he would not let me go. Gyaltsap Rinpoche assured him that I would be of benefit to the teachings and to all beings, so my father agreed to let me go. However, I was then still too young to be sent to Shechen.

"Just before Mipham Rinpoche died he told Lama Ösel, his lifelong attendant and disciple, 'When I die you will feel great pain, but not for long.' After Mipham Rinpoche's death, Lama Ösel almost went insane. He starved himself and kept going restlessly in and out of his room. After a hundred days he had a vision in which he saw Mipham Rinpoche in the sky, wearing a *pandita*'s hat and writing a text. As he finished each page he threw it down to Lama Ösel. The letters he wrote were not in black ink but in brilliant golden light. Lama Ösel looked at one of the pages and could read a few words, 'Ösel . . . Jalu . . . Dorje . . . Radiant light . . . rainbow body . . . adamantine. . . .' Then Mipham Rinpoche

(above) *A* **Rishi** *meditating in a cave.*
(below) *The cave of the great sage Padampa Sangye, in which Khyentse Rinpoche spent many months in retreat* (see page 40).

gestured toward the sky and said three times, 'Ösel Jalu Dorje!' From then on, Lama Ösel's sadness totally disappeared.

"A short while later, I was taken to see Kunzang Dechen Dorje, a highly accomplished master. He said, 'This child and I have known each other before,' and asked me, 'Do you know me?'

"'Do you know him?' repeated my father.

"'Yes, I know him,' I said, a bit scared.

"Kunzang Dechen Dorje said, 'For many previous lives we have had a connection. I am going to give him a fine present.' He had a rare and cherished collection of cups. Gold, silver, and other possessions were of no interest to him, but he treasured his cups. He said to his wife, 'Bring my box of cups,' and presented me with an exquisite cup, which he filled with raisins.

"My father told Dechen Dorje that we were going on pilgrimage to Lhasa and asked for his protection.

"'I will pray for you,' he said. 'Usually I forget whom I'm supposed to include in my prayers unless my wife reminds me—but I'll never forget this child.'

"We traveled to Lhasa on pilgrimage. There, another lama, Taklung Matrul, told my father, 'You should look after this child very carefully because he must be an incarnate lama.'

"My father said nothing. But when we came back to our lodgings, he declared, 'The lamas won't let me keep this son, but I'm not going to let him become a lama. We have a large family, an estate, and much land to look after. I want him to stay a layman so that he can take care of it all.'

"When we returned to Kham, my father, my eldest brother Shedrup, and myself met the great teacher Adzom Drukpa. He was a very impressive man. He wore a white raw silk shirt with a collar of red brocade and had a chain of onyx round his neck. He had long black hair with a touch of silver, tied up on top of his head with a scarf. He inquired if I were the son who would hold the family estates, for I was wearing a layman's robe and wore my long hair wound around my head in Derge style.

"Then he laughed and said, 'Yes, in a way he will hold the family estates. But there is a big obstacle. Shall I look for it?' My father assented.

"A moment later, Adzom Drukpa said, 'It would be better if you made him a monk.'

"My father replied that making me a monk would be very difficult.

"'Then I'll dispel the obstacle,' said Adzom Drukpa.

"A symbolic arrow of longevity was brought, and they measured its length. Adzom Drukpa recited a long life invocation, and they measured the arrow again. It had shrunk in length by a finger-span.

"'There,' said Adzom Drukpa, 'that is the obstacle I told you about!'

"My father did not seem particularly impressed. Adzom Drukpa recited the invocation three more times, and pulled on the arrow. Once again, they measured it, and this time it was longer than it had been at the outset.

"'I'm not just an ordinary man,' said Adzom Drukpa, 'and I repeat that it would be better if you made him a monk.'

"But my father still did not react. Every day for seven days, Adzom Drukpa gave me a long-life blessing. On the last day he announced, 'Now I have dispelled the obstacle.'

"Soon afterward we returned home, with no further comment about my becoming a monk.

"On the way back to Denkhok we met Dzogchen Rinpoche, who was presiding over a picnic by the large rock in front of Dzogchen Monastery. He, too, said that I would have obstacles and that to counteract them we should save the lives of animals. We returned home, and since my father owned many animals we were able to save several thousand sheep, yaks, and goats from slaughter.

"That same year I was burnt by the soup. Summer on our estate was the busiest time of the agricultural year, during which we employed many workers. To feed them all, huge quantities of soup were cooked in an enormous cauldron. One day, playing with my brother, I fell into the cauldron of boiling soup. The lower half of my body was so badly scalded that I was bedridden for many months, seriously ill despite the many long-life prayers that my family recited for me.

"My father asked me in desperation, 'What ceremonies do you think will help you get better? If there's anything that can save your life, we must do it!'

"What I wanted most was to be a monk, so I replied, 'It would help if I could wear monk's robes.' My father gave his word, and quickly got some robes made. When I had them laid over me in bed, I felt overjoyed. I also had placed on my pillow a bell and ritual hand drum.

"The very next day I asked Lama Ösel to come and shave my head. I was told that a few of our old retainers wept that day, lamenting, 'Now the last Dilgo son has taken vows, that's the end of the family line.' But I was so happy that soon my health improved, and the risk of an untimely death receded. I was then ten years old."

The view from White Grove, some five hours' walk into the wilderness from Khyentse Rinpoche's birthplace, Sakar, in the valley of Denkhok. Here stood a wooden hut, where Khyentse Rinpoche spent four years in retreat (see pages 41–43). The hut, which no longer exists, was so tiny that there was no room for more than one person to sit inside.

A typical landscape of rolling pasture and moorland in Eastern Tibet. In the foreground is a nomad family's yak-hair tent, suspended from external tent poles. The tent has a hole in the center to let out the smoke from a fire of dried dung that burns day and night in the hearth. A typical summer camp consists of four or five such tents, inhabited by an extended family group that herds several hundred sheep and yaks. Nomad groups maintain a close connection with a monastery, in this case Shechen; generally one or two sons from each generation join the monastery. One son born in this camp became a monk in Shechen Monastery in Nepal and is now the monastery's computer specialist for Tibetan word processing.

When might I abide in such a place,
A place unclaimed, by nature ownerless,
That's wide and unconfined, a place where I might stay
At liberty without attachment?

In solitude, the mind and body
Are not troubled by distraction.
Therefore, leave this worldly life
And totally abandon mental wandering.

Penetrative insight joined with calm abiding
Utterly eradicates afflicted states.
Knowing this, first search for calm abiding,
Found by those who joyfully renounce the world.

Therefore in these lovely gleaming woods,
With joy that's marred by few afflictions,
I shall pacify all mental wandering,
And there remain in blissful solitude.

In pleasant dwellings formed of massive stone,
And cooled by sandal trees beneath the moon,
In woodlands wafted by the gentle breeze,
Our minds intent on bringing good to others.

Those whose minds are practiced in this way
Whose happiness it is to soothe the pain of others,
Will venture in the hell of unremitting agony
As swans sweep down upon a lotus lake.

The oceanlike immensity of joy
Arising when all beings will be freed,
Will this not be enough? Will this not satisfy?
The wish for my own freedom, what is that to me?

Shantideva

A group of Khampa horsemen gallop through the meadowland alongside Khyentse Rinpoche's car. Khampas are among the most skillful horsemen in the world; the horse is an essential and everyday means of transport for everybody, even young children.

As the mountain torrent flows toward the ocean,
As sun and moon sink closer to the mountains in the west,
As days, and nights, and hours, and minutes pass so quickly by—
Just so, inexorably, a human life runs out.

Padmasambhava

Life flickers in the flurries of a thousand ills,
More fragile than a bubble in a stream.
In sleep, each breath departs and is again drawn in;
How wondrous that we wake up living still!

Nagarjuna

Like a flickering star, a mirage, or a flame,
Like a magical illusion, a dewdrop, or a bubble on a stream,
Like a dream, a flash of lightning, or a cloud—
See all compounded things as being like these.

Chandrakirti

From bird song and the sighing of the trees,
From shafts of light and from the sky itself,
May living beings, each and every one,
Perceive the constant sound of Dharma.

Shantideva

All the joy the world contains
Has come through wishing happiness for others.
All the misery the world contains
Has come through wanting pleasure for oneself.

Shantideva

Fearing death, I went to the mountains.
Over and over again I meditated on death's unpredictable coming,
And took the stronghold of the deathless unchanging nature.
Now I am completely beyond all fear of dying!

Milarepa

My native land is all lands—in no particular direction.

My monastery is the solitary mountains—in no particular place.

My family is all beings of the six realms.

My name is "Hermit Protected by the Three Jewels."

Shabkar

(opposite) *Shechen Monastery in Eastern Tibet. The main building, razed to the ground during the Cultural Revolution, is now half rebuilt, and is surrounded by small houses of mud blocks and wood, built and inhabited by the monks— typically an uncle with several nephews who are his pupils and charges.*

Above the monastery to the right is the three-year retreat center and, higher still, Shechen Gyaltsap Rinpoche's hermitage. On top of the hill to the left stand the ruins of Shechen Kongtrul Rinpoche's retreat house (see page 33).

The tents below near the banks of the river are those of lamas and monks who made long journeys to meet Khyentse Rinpoche during his visit.

(right) *Two monks who have come to welcome Khyentse Rinpoche. The mounted one was the principal attendant of the former abbot, Shechen Rabjam, who died of starvation in a Chinese prison; the other is the monastery's chant master. Both were prisoners in a hard-labor camp for more than fifteen years, and have only been allowed to wear their monastic robes again in the last few years.*

The two-day annual festival of sacred dance at Shechen Monastery. The dances celebrate the coming of the great Guru Padmasambhava, who brought Buddhism to Tibet in the eighth *century. The entire community of two hundred and fifty monks takes part in the event. The dances are also attended by all the nomads of the region, for whom this is the year's major festivity.*

A monk plays a large skin drum during the sacred dance festival. He wears a thick body-length sheepskin mantle, even in July, when, although it is the warmest month of the year, there may be snowfalls. His winter dress includes a much thicker cloak, made from several large sheep-skins sewn together. Tibetans find the sight of Westerners wearing coats with the fur outside hilarious.

Hundreds of monks work in orchestrated teams to pitch the vast tent in which the sacred dance festival will take place.

The thick white cotton has been stitched together over a week by some fifteen monks.

Following the main two-day festival, two further days of festivities are held in the open air near the river. The monks picnic and sleep in tents. The first day's ceremonies and dances include offerings of fragrant incense smoke to the local deities to ensure the prosperity of the monastery and its surrounding lay community.

Kyema! Kyehu! My dearest parents,
You gave me birth with all the freedoms and advantages of
    human life,
And you have cared for me with love, from my infancy till now.
Since you introduced me to an authentic teacher,
It is thanks to your kindness that I have encountered the path
    of liberation.

After hearing, thinking about, and meditating on
The life of my perfect teacher,
I have resolved to slip quietly away from all this life's concerns
And roam through empty, uninhabited valleys.

Father and mother, stay in your handsome, lofty house;
I, your young son, long instead for empty caves.

Thank you for the fine, soft clothes you gave me;
Yet I don't need them—I would rather dress in plain white felt.

I leave my valuable belongings behind—
A begging bowl, a staff, and Dharma robes are all I need.

*On the first day of the main festival, the monks rehearse in plain
monastic dress, adding some simple yellow scarves. Only on the second
day will they wear their complete costumes of brocade and their wooden
masks. A large crowd of fervent lay spectators has already gathered.*

I've cast aside this luxury and wealth with no regrets;
A handbook of profound advice is all I wish to collect.

I leave this garden full of splendid flowers,
And head for the wilderness of overhanging cliffs alone.

I need no attendants, who just fuel anger and attachment:
Birds and wild animals are the only company I long for.

Earlier, in the presence of my sovereign teacher,
As he bestowed the *Secret Heart Essence* empowerment,
I vowed to abandon all the activities of this life
And practice in accordance with the Dharma.
In my heart that promise is as clear as if engraved in stone—
I cannot but leave for a secluded mountain retreat.

Although for now your son will hide away in mountain glens,
Your smiling faces will be with me always,
Nor shall I forget your loving care;
And if I reach the citadel of experience and realization,
I shall repay your kindness, of that you can be sure!

written by Khyentse Rinpoche when he was thirteen years old

Fragrant juniper smoke rises from the scene of the first day of the open-air dances in front of the main ritual tent, with its fifty-meter guy-ropes of yak hair. All around, visitors' horses graze freely until the time comes for each person to identify his own mount from afar—with uncanny accuracy—before riding home.

This photograph, taken in 1995, shows the progress made in the rebuilding of the monastery, compared to photographs taken in 1985 (page 113) when the entire monastery was still in ruins, and in 1988 (such as pages 20 and 108–109).

Just as every single thing is always moving inexorably closer to its ultimate dissolution, so also your own life, like a burning butter-lamp, will soon be consumed. It would be foolish to think that you can first finish all your work and then retire to spend the later stages of your life practicing the Dharma. Can you be certain that you will live that long? Does death not strike the young as well as the old? No matter what you are doing, therefore, remember death and keep your mind focused on the Dharma.

Khyentse Rinpoche

Butter can be made by churning milk because the fat is already present in the milk; no one has ever made butter by churning water. A gold digger looks for gold in rocks, not in wood. In just the same way, striving to attain Buddhahood makes sense because the Buddha-nature is inherent in sentient beings. Were it not for that potential, any such effort would be a waste of time.

Jamgön Kongtrul

While a sailor has a boat, he should cross the ocean; while a commander has a company of brave men gathered together, he should defeat the enemy; while a poor man has a wish-granting cow, he should milk it; while a traveler has a superb horse, he should ride it to faraway places. Now, while you have a precious human life and a teacher who embodies the Buddhas of past, present and future, think with great joy and enthusiasm how you will travel the highway of the sacred Dharma, drawing ever closer to the ultimate goal of liberation and enlightenment.

Shabkar

Local nomads in their thick sheepskins wait by the roadside amidst clouds of incense smoke to welcome Khyentse Rinpoche to Shechen after thirty years of exile.

A young monk circumambulates a huge wall of flat stones, each entirely covered with hand-carved prayers and mantras. The wall is topped with prayer flags. In East-ern Tibet there were several examples of walls containing the whole Buddhist Canon carved in stone—the equivalent of 103 thick books. They were all dismantled and scattered by the Chinese. A team of Shechen monks is currently carving the entire canon again.

A nomad family in their summer pastures, which, paradoxically, are often at lower altitude than winter grazing land; in the valleys, the thick winter snow is impenetrable, whereas on the mountain slopes high winds keep the snow thinner, allowing the starving yaks a little meager grazing. Calving time is in early summer, the only season in which the dri (the female of the yak) can graze enough to feed her young.

MEETING SPIRITUAL TEACHERS

Khyentse Rinpoche's predecessor, Jamyang Khyentse Wangpo (1820–1892), spent thirteen years traveling tirelessly all over Tibet to receive thousands of different traditions and lineages of Buddhist practice, many of them on the verge of extinction. He traveled modestly on foot with a pack on his back—wearing out, so it is said, three pairs of boots. Having gathered these important teachings together, Khyentse Wangpo and another great master, Jamgön Kongtrul, painstakingly edited, arranged, and published them in five great collections. They then set about transmitting to their students the oral explanation and ritual empowerments accompanying these texts, the living tradition without which the books alone would have retained only a symbolic value for future generations.[1] By thus preserving so many precious teachings, Khyentse Wangpo became the instigator of a veritable Buddhist renaissance throughout Tibet—a movement from which many contemporary Tibetan masters still draw inspiration. At the age of forty, he went into retreat for the rest of his life, never emerging from his hermitage until his death at the age of seventy-three.

Dzongsar Khyentse Chökyi Lodrö (1896–1959), Khyentse Rinpoche's second main teacher.

Madhyamika ('middle way') philosophy. In the morning I would receive teachings from him and study on my own. In the afternoon I would answer his questions on the subjects he had taught that morning and repeat a few pages of the texts I was meant to have learned by heart. Some afternoons he would take me outdoors to play. Once he showed me how to lob little pebbles at a rock in front of his hut, making the field voles that were bustling around it scurry away; he was very good at it. He wanted to keep me entertained so that I would not get bored with my studies.

"A little later Khenpo Shenga left for the Rainbow Light Cave in Derge, where he lived like Milarepa in strict retreat. I followed and stayed there with him for five months, receiving further teachings, including Patrul Rinpoche's *The Words of My Perfect Teacher*. One day he said to me, 'Look at the nature of mind, and tell me how it is.' Not far from our tents, at the foot of a cliff, was a pleasant meadow. I sat there to meditate, and it appeared to me that the nature of mind was empty and clear. I reported this to Khenpo Shenga, and both he and the great hermit Kunga Palden were pleased; they interpreted it as proof of my having practiced in previous lives. But I thought that I must have arrived at this answer conceptually through my Madhyamika studies, and doubted that I had directly experienced the ultimate nature of mind.

To the northeast of Derge lies Shechen, one of the six principal monasteries of the Nyingmapa school. It was there that Khyentse Wangpo's close disciple Shechen Gyaltsap Rinpoche (1871–1926) formally recognized and enthroned the young Dilgo Khyentse Rinpoche as one of the five incarnations of this extraordinarily great lama. The boy was then twelve years old. Khyentse Rinpoche tells of those golden years he spent with his teachers:

"Some time after my return home, my elder brother, Shedrup, said to me that study was all very well but theoretical knowledge on its own was not enough. His advice was to seek out a teacher with the highest realization. In his view, the most accomplished teacher then alive was Shechen Gyaltsap Rinpoche. My other brother, Sangye Nyenpa Rinpoche, had just finished a three-year retreat and wanted to meet Gyaltsap Rinpoche too. So the three of us, along with my father and ten other people, set out for Shechen.

"After I had become a novice monk at the age of ten, a great scholar named Khenpo Shenga came to Denkhok on his way to Kyerku, where he was building a monastic college. He felt that I was the reincarnation of his teacher, Onpo Tenga, who had also been my father's root teacher. He said I should come to his monastic college, where he would teach me. So I went to Kyerku and received detailed teachings from him on *The Way of the Bodhisattva* and on

"When we arrived, Gyaltsap Rinpoche's attendant greeted us with two ceremonial scarves, one for myself and one for Nyenpa Rinpoche. He conveyed Gyaltsap Rinpoche's wish that the two of us wait for an auspicious date to meet

Shechen Kongtrul (1901–1960) (left), and Shechen Gyaltsap (1871–1926) (right), Khyentse Rinpoche's first main teacher.

him, for it would be the first time we had ever met him at Shechen. Shedrup, however, having been there before, could visit him whenever he wished.

"We waited for three days before receiving word; and to me, waiting to meet my teacher for the first time, those days seemed very long. At long last we were taken up to his retreat quarters. Gyaltsap Rinpoche was wearing a yellow jacket lined with fur, instead of monastic robes. His hair, curling at the ends, had grown long enough to fall around his shoulders, for he rarely left his retreat hermitage. We were seated and served sweet saffron rice. Gyaltsap Rinpoche wanted to know all about the teachers Nyenpa Rinpoche had met and the teachings he had received. Nyenpa Rinpoche answered his questions for about three hours.

"Gyaltsap Rinpoche's hermitage was perched on a spur of the mountainside about forty-five minutes' walk above Shechen Monastery. The path up to this beautiful spot was quite steep, and slippery during the rainy season. From the window you could see the monastery and the river down below in the valley, framed all around by mountains snow-covered for most of the year. Just below the hermitage was a platform among juniper bushes, ideal for sitting quietly on sunny days. Lower down was a small cave called the Cave of Luminous Great Bliss, in which Gyaltsap Rinpoche had spent some months in retreat. Above the

[1] In the Tibetan tradition, if one is going to study or practice a text one should first listen to it being read aloud by a lama who himself heard it from his teacher. Often initiatory rituals called "empowerments" must also be given, as well as the oral explanation of the text.

hermitage were more caves; in one, sacred images seemed to have formed spontaneously in the rock face. Halfway down towards the monastery was Shechen's main retreat center, where nearly twenty monks at a time would practice the traditional three-year, three-month, and three-day retreat.

"Gyaltsap Rinpoche was indisputably one of the most learned and accomplished lamas of his time. Once he started a three-year retreat, but after only three months—to everyone's surprise—he emerged, saying that he had completed his intended program. The next morning, his attendant noticed that a footprint had appeared in the stone threshold of his hermitage. That stone was later removed by disciples and kept hidden during the Cultural Revolution; it can still be seen nowadays at Shechen Monastery (see picture below).

"The monastery used to house more than two hundred monks. Their abbot was Shechen Rabjam Rinpoche, another of my principal teachers, and it was he who used to instruct the monks and give them empowerments. He also visited other monasteries to teach, traveling extensively as far as Central Tibet.

"Also at Shechen was a third great lama, Shechen Kongtrul Rinpoche. He lived on the other side of the mountain torrent from Gyaltsap Rinpoche's hermitage, on the flat top of another promontory in the mountainside—a delightful place of meadows covered in summer with yellow flowers, and of thick fir forests where delicious mushrooms were to be found. Shechen Kongtrul was a great meditator and, like Shechen Gyaltsap, took no part in the monastery's administration, which was looked after by Shechen Rabjam.

"One day we were called up to Gyaltsap Rinpoche's hermitage. When we arrived he told us that his teachings would begin that day, and the very first empowerment would be for the practice of Vajrasattva according to the Mindroling tradition. Throughout the following months, he gave us all the most important teachings from the Nyingma Canon, the transmission of Mipham Rinpoche's *Complete Works*, and the *Four-Part Heart Essence* of the great Nyingma master Longchen Rabjam. After the teachings I would often go to see Shechen Gyaltsap Rinpoche. He was fond of children and he seemed to enjoy joking and playing around with me. He was always gentle and considerate, and throughout his life hardly ever got angry. During long teachings, he would make a point of playing with the young lamas and telling them stories.

"While he was giving empowerments, I was often overwhelmed by the splendor and magnificence of his expression and his eyes as, with a gesture pointing in my direction, he introduced the nature of mind. I felt that, apart from my own feeble devotion that made me see the teacher as an ordinary man, this was in fact exactly the same as the great Guru Padmasambhava him-

Shechen Gyaltsap's footprint in the rock (see text).

self giving empowerments to the twenty-five disciples. My confidence grew stronger and stronger, and when again he would gaze and point at me, asking, 'What is the nature of mind?,' I would think with great devotion, 'This is truly a great yogi who can see the absolute nature of reality!' and began to understand, myself, how to meditate.

"On my next visit to Shechen, I received ordination as a novice monk from Gyaltsap Rinpoche. Khenpo Shenga had already given me these vows once, but I told Gyaltsap Rinpoche that I would like to receive them again from him. He replied that it was legitimate to receive vows twice, just as a stupa can be embellished with several layers of gold.

The sixth Shechen Rabjam (1910–1959), abbot of Shechen Monastery, whose present incarnation, the seventh, is Khyentse Rinpoche's grandson.

"When Dzongsar Khyentse Chökyi Lodrö had first spoken to Gyaltsap Rinpoche about me, he had said: 'I have met this child before and I feel strongly that he is an incarnation of Jamyang Khyentse Wangpo. Please take care of him, and I too will do whatever I can to serve him. In particular, I beg you to transmit to him the *Treasury of Instructions.*' This was the transmission that Gyaltsap Rinpoche decided to give next. These were teachings for serious practitioners only, he said, and while giving them he would see only those people he had selected as ready to receive the empowerments. He made a list of about twenty of us, and put a sign up near the door to mark the boundaries of the retreat. The *Treasury* contains teachings from all eight main schools of Tibetan Buddhism. As Gyaltsap Rinpoche taught, his voice was not very strong, but it was clear and I could understand everything he said. I still remember it in my old age. I really consider him my root teacher, for it was he who introduced to me the nature of mind.

"Khyentse Chökyi Lodrö had a copy of the books and I was told to follow the text with him. At one point, Gyaltsap Rinpoche was taken ill for a while, and during that period Khyentse Chökyi Lodrö gave a reading transmission of some other teachings. Gyaltsap Rinpoche recovered in his room, from which—thanks to a window communicating with the small shrine hall in which we gathered—he was able to take part in the proceedings. I sat next to his window and was asked, as I listened to the reading, to correct his copy of the text. It was wonderful to have the opportunity of seeing him every day and working with him on these books. Sometimes, Khyentse Chökyi Lodrö told me to write some poems.

Although I was very young, I did quite well; Gyaltsap Rinpoche was very pleased and said that I would become a good writer.

"Altogether the teachings took three months. At the end we performed two days of thanksgiving ceremonies—including a large feast offering with Gyaltsap Rinpoche himself as the chant master, a unique occasion.

"After concluding these teachings, Gyaltsap Rinpoche enthroned me as the incarnation of Jamyang Khyentse Wangpo's mind. Khyentse Wangpo had five incarnations, who were respectively the emanations of his body, speech, mind, qualities, and activity. Khyentse Chökyi Lodrö was the incarnation of his activity.

"On the morning of the enthronement I climbed up the path to the hermitage. Inside, a large throne had been set up. Shechen Kongtrul, who was still very young then, was holding incense, and Shechen Gyaltsap was dressed in his finest clothes. They told me to sit on the throne. Only a few people were present in the room. They chanted verses describing the sacred qualities of the time and place of a teaching, of the teacher, of what he teaches, and of those who receive his teaching. Gyaltsap Rinpoche performed the ceremony and made me precious gifts symbolic of the body, speech, mind, qualities, and activity of the Buddhas. As symbol of body, he gave me images of Buddha Shakyamuni that had belonged to Mipham Rinpoche and Jamyang Khyentse Wangpo. As symbol of speech, he gave me many volumes of their writings. As symbol of mind, he gave me the *vajra* and the bell that Mipham Rinpoche had used throughout his life. As symbol of qualities, he gave me all the articles necessary for giving empowerments. Finally, as symbol of activity, he gave me Mipham Rinpoche's seal. Then he presented me with a written document, which said: 'Today I take the son of the Dilgo family and recognize him as the re-embodiment of Jamyang Khyentse Wangpo. I name him Gyurme Thekchog Tenpai Gyaltsen, Immutable Victory Banner of the Supreme Vehicle. I entrust him with the teachings of the great masters of the past. Now, if I die I have no regret.'

"So these, and other occasions over a period of about five years, were the times I spent with Gyaltsap Rinpoche at Shechen. While there, I lived not in the monastery itself but at the retreat center up the hill.

"Then I went back home. I stayed in retreat for about a year in a cave called Boyam Samphutri. During the winter, without coming out of retreat, I asked the learned Khenpo Thubga to come and give me detailed teachings on the *Tantra of the Secret Quintessence.* He went through it three times altogether, and I learned by heart both the root text and Longchenpa's three-hundred-page commentary.

"Some time later, I went to Kyangma Ritrö, where Khenpo Thubga lived. There was no monastery or other buildings there, only tents. It was there, at the age of fifteen, that I learned in a letter from my father that Gyaltsap Rinpoche had died. For a moment my mind went blank. Then, suddenly, the memory of my teacher arose so strongly in my mind that I was overwhelmed and wept. That day I felt as if my heart had been torn from my chest. I went back to Denkhok and started a period of retreat in the mountains that would last for thirteen years."

Dzongshö Deshek Düpa, the retreat place of the first Jamgön Kongtrul (1813–1899), midway between Dzongsar and Kathog. In the crags around the site are nine large caves in which he and Jamyang Khyentse Wangpo discovered many "spiritual treasures" (see page 70). In the main hermitage, Jamgön Kongtrul compiled the Collection of Revealed Treasures, a sixty-three-volume collection of spiritual treasures from the eleventh century onwards.

(top, left to right) *Mañjushri, Buddha of Wisdom, severs the root of ignorance with his sword. The Khyentse incarnations are considered to be emanations of Mañjushri.*

As Shakyamuni sits under the Bodhi tree on the eve of his enlightenment, the devil Mara—the personification of the ego—unleashes his last assault. He first sends his three daughters to distract him with their sensual beauty. But the moment they approach him, their faces and bodies wither into senility. Mara then conjures up his magical armies, which whirl around Shakyamuni like a storm, shouting insults and hurling weapons at him. Had the future Buddha had a single angry thought, he would have been crushed into dust. But his whole being is pervaded by love and compassion, and the rain of weapons turns into a rain of flowers, the deluge of insults into a shower of praises.

As the night advances, Shakyamuni's meditation deepens until, as the morning star appears, he knows he has attained the ultimate goal. He is now the Buddha, the Awakened One.

(left) *Some strong men are trying to remove a huge boulder sunk into the ground. The Buddha happens to pass by, and tells them, "Your efforts have come to nothing, and even if you had succeeded, what would you have gained?" So saying, he uproots the boulder with his toe, and takes it in his right hand. He blows on it and the boulder is shattered into dust. A strong wind arises and its roaring voice declares: "All compounded things are impermanent; thereby are illusions brought to nothing. Phenomena are empty of self; peace is found in nirvana alone."*

As recorded in the Sutra of Final Nirvana *and other texts, shortly before passing into nirvana, Buddha Shakyamuni prophesied that, since in this life he had not taught the esoteric teachings of the tantras extensively, he would return to the world after twelve years, taking a miraculous birth, in order to expound the tantric teachings. This rebirth was Guru Padmasambhava, the Lotus Born Guru, who emanated from the heart of the Buddha Amitabha and miraculously appeared in the form of an eight-year-old child upon a lotus, at Danakosha Lake in Oddiyana (top left). Having studied with the eight "awareness-holders" of India, such as Humchenkara (center) and Prabhahasti (right)—seen here giving him a tantric empowerment in the Red Rock Garuda cave—he achieved ultimate enlightenment at Asura Cave in Nepal. He was invited by the King of Tibet to establish Buddhism in the Land of Snows. On his way he subdued evil forces and spirits, whose attacks took many forms, including an attempt to crush him between collapsing mountains. But Padmasambhava flew into the sky (left) and with a symbolic gesture held the mountains apart.*

In the eighth century, King Trisong Detsen (top left) *invited Guru Padmasambhava* (top center), *revered as the second Buddha, to establish the first monastery in Tibet, at Samye* (see page 126) *on the advice of the Abbot Shantarakshita* (top right). *Guru Padmasambhava also had the canonical Buddhist scriptures translated by 108 Tibetan translators working with the same number of Indian scholars. He gave countless empowerments related to the path of the Tantras. In most instances, after giving a particular teach-ing, he had it concealed in a rock, a lake, a statue, etc., by a close disciple, often the Dakini Yeshe Tsogyal* (left), *and estab-lished a prophecy detailing how in the future that "spiritual treasure" would be revealed by an incarnation of one of his disciples, who would then propagate it for the benefit of beings* (see page 70).

Despite a period of intense persecution (841–46 A.D.*) by King Langdarma, Buddhism flourished in Tibet. New waves of translations brought more scriptures from India in the eleventh century, and numerous schools bloomed, following the appearance of many remarkable saints and scholars. Principal among these schools are the "eight great chariots of spiritual accomplishment." From these, four main traditions emerged—Nyingma, Kagyu, Sakya, and Geluk—which continue to this day to foster the rich contemplative and philosophical heritage of Tibet.*

A crystal takes on the color of the cloth upon which it is placed, whether white, yellow, red, or black. Likewise, the people you spend your time with, whether their influence is good or bad, will make a huge difference to the direction your life and practice take.

Spending your time with true spiritual friends will fill you with love for all beings and help you to see how negative attachment and hatred are. Being with such friends, and following their example, will naturally imbue you with their good qualities, just as all the birds flying around a golden mountain are bathed in its golden radiance.

To free yourself from samsara, the vicious circle of suffering existence, and attain the omniscience of enlightenment, you have to rely on an authentic teacher. Such a teacher always thinks, speaks, and acts in perfect accord with the Dharma. He shows you what to do to make progress on the path, and what obstacles to avoid. An authentic spiritual teacher is like the sail that enables a boat to cross the ocean swiftly.

If you trust his words, you will find your way out of samsara easily; that is why the teacher is considered so precious. Enlightenment is not something that can be accomplished just by following your own ideas; each separate stage of your practice, whether based on the sutras or tantras, requires an explanation from a qualified teacher.

It is said that the Buddhas of the past, those of the present, and those to come have all achieved or will achieve Buddhahood by following a teacher.

The Buddha's teaching is immense, its transmissions are numerous, and it covers an inexhaustible range of topics. Without following a teacher's pith instructions, we would never know how to condense all those teachings down to the most essential points and put them into practice.

Although the teacher appears to us in ordinary human form, and seems to behave in an ordinary human way, in reality his mind is no different from the Buddha's. The only difference between the teacher and the Buddha lies in his kindness to you, which in fact exceeds that of all the Buddhas of the past—for though they were perfectly enlightened, you can neither meet them in person nor hear their teachings. Your spiritual teacher, on the other hand, has come into this world in your time. You can meet him and receive from him the instructions that will lead you out of the mire of samsara to enlightenment.

Khyentse Rinpoche

THE DEPTH OF SPIRITUAL PRACTICE

Shechen Gyaltsap had given the young Khyentse Rinpoche numerous teachings, and had opened his mind to its true nature. Khyentse Rinpoche had promised his beloved master that he, in turn, would show the same unstinting generosity to those who asked him for instruction. So in order to first prepare himself—he was only fifteen when Shechen Gyaltsap died—he spent most of the next thirteen years in silent retreat. In remote hermitages and caves deep in the steep wilderness of wooded hills near his birthplace in the valley of Denkhok, he constantly meditated on love, compassion, and the wish to bring all sentient beings to freedom and enlightenment. Khyentse Rinpoche tells us about the years he spent in retreat:

Mount Bahla, dominating the valley of Denkhok, at the foot of whose high crags is a cave in which Khyentse Rinpoche spent a whole winter snowbound in solitary retreat.

"I practiced from the early hours before dawn until noon, and from afternoon late into the night. At midday I read from my books, reciting the texts aloud to learn them by heart. I stayed in a cave at Cliff Hermitage for seven years, at White Grove (see page 15) for three years, and in other caves and huts for a few months at a time, surrounded by thick forests and snow mountains.

"Not far from the Padampa caves (see page 14) was a cottage, where my brother Shedrup and two attendants made food. My cave had no door, and small bears used to come and snuffle around the entrance. But they were unable to climb the ladder into the cave. Outside in the forest lived foxes and all sorts of birds. There were leopards not very far away, too; they caught a small dog I had with me. A cuckoo lived nearby, and he was my alarm clock. As soon as I heard him, around three o'clock in the morning, I would get up and start a session of meditation. At five o'clock I made myself some tea, which meant that I had no need to see anyone until lunchtime. In the evening I would let the fire go out slowly so that next morning the embers were still hot enough to be stoked up again. I could revive the fire and boil tea in my one big pot without getting up from my seat, just by leaning forward. I had a large number of books with me. The cave was quite roomy—high enough to stand up in without hitting my head on the roof—but slightly damp. Like most caves, it was cool in summer and retained some warmth in winter.

"I lived in the cave at Cliff Hermitage without coming out of retreat for seven years. My parents would come to see me from time to time. I was sixteen when I started that retreat. I sat all the time in a four-sided wooden box, occasionally stretching my legs out. Shedrup, my elder brother, was my retreat teacher, and he told me that unless I sometimes took a walk outside I might end up quite deranged; but I felt not the slightest wish to go out. Shedrup was practicing, too, in partial retreat in a hut nearby. With him was an attendant who from time to time went to fetch provisions from our house, three hours away by horse. When I returned to Kham in 1985, I met that attendant again, still alive.

"Many small birds ventured into my cave. If I put some butter on the tip of my finger, they would come and peck at it. I also shared the cave with two mice. I fed them with barley flour, and they used to run around on my lap. Crows would carry off the offerings I put outside.

"For five or six years I ate no meat. For three years I did not speak a single word. At noon, after lunch, I used to relax a little and study some books; I never wasted time doing nothing at all. My brother Shedrup often encouraged me to compose prayers, spiritual songs, and poems, which he thought would give me practice in writing. I found it easy to write, and by the end of that period I had written about a thousand pages; but later, when we fled Tibet, it was all lost.

"That cave had a very clear feeling about it, and there were no distractions. I let my hair grow and it got very long. When I practiced 'inner warmth' I experienced a lot of heat, and day and night for years, in spite of the very cold climate, I wore only a white shawl and a robe of raw silk. I sat on a bearskin. Outside everything was frozen solid, but inside the cave was warm.

"Later, I moved to White Grove. There I made myself a small wooden hut with one small window. I often saw wolves panting by; sometimes they would stop to rub themselves against the corner of the hut. There were also many deer and blue sheep, and occasionally I saw leopards. Once a month my mother came to see me, and stayed for an hour to talk."

During this period, Khyentse Rinpoche became seriously ill. Khyentse Chökyi Lodrö and many other lamas were of the unanimous opinion that the time had come for him to take a consort, as was necessary for him as a *tertön*, or finder of spiritual treasures (texts concealed by Guru Padmasambhava to be revealed by specific individuals in future times). So he married Lhamo, a simple girl from an ordinary farming family. From then on his health improved; he had many deep visions and revealed several mind treasures. His wife, Khandro Lhamo, recalls those times:

"I was living at home with my mother. One day she sent me to work in the fields. On the way, I met some lamas who told me they had come to take me somewhere. I said I had no time, as my mother had told me to go and work. But they explained that I was to accompany them to where Khyentse Rinpoche was in retreat. Nowadays the Chinese have felled all the trees, but in those days it meant traveling through dense forest, and I was scared of the wild animals.

"Rinpoche's hermitage was a tiny wooden hut. His brother, Apo Shedrup, lived nearby in another small cabin, and I had a separate little cottage. The kitchen was further down the hill, in a small, open cave. With our two servants, there were five of us there altogether.

"Rinpoche was very ill and his face looked dark. I was worried to see him so sick and thought he was going to die. But after my arrival his health seemed to improve. One day he was up and about in his white robe, and he asked me to come and eat with him.

"When I first came to live with Rinpoche, Khyentse Chökyi Lodrö and other lamas had told him to get married to prolong his life, otherwise he would die. In some texts it was predicted that Rinpoche should marry me, to ensure that his activities for the Buddhadharma would become very vast. One prediction I heard said something like this:

The young yogi with an A on his forehead
From the virtuous family of Sakar mansion,
To prolong his life, should wed the maiden born in the Wood Tiger year.

"Rinpoche himself did not seem the slightest bit interested in having a wife. He did not care whether he died or not, he said; he only got married because his teacher had told him to. Later, I jokingly scolded Apo Shedrup and the other lamas for not having told me I was to be Rinpoche's consort. At least I would have been able to get ready and put on something nice—instead of the scruffy old working clothes in which they had brought me there. They laughed, and said they had deliberately not told me, for fear that I might think about it and refuse to come.

"Rinpoche's retreat hut was very simple. The walls were plastered with mud, and he had a wooden box to sit in. He was always asking for books, which I used to fetch back and forth for him. There were too many books to fit in his room, so some had to be kept somewhere else. When the books were new, the cloth they were wrapped in had been white; but he had used them so much that the cloth had turned brown. The inside of the hut was so small and full of books that there was no place for the shrine, which had to be outside on a small veranda. Next to it I planted many flowers in pots, which Rinpoche liked very much.

"Down at the river near the retreat place, Rinpoche had left a footprint in the rock. It was found by one of the servants, who used to go down there to get milk, curd, and butter from the herdsmen. They were sure it had not been there before Rinpoche started his retreat. Pema Shepa saw another footprint that Rinpoche left later, while he was on pilgrimage with Khyentse Chökyi Lodrö. Not knowing how to make new boots, I had myself patched the boots Rinpoche was wearing at the time, and the patch in the boot was quite visible in the clear footprint. Goka also saw it and told us about it, but Rinpoche denied that it was his.

"At night, when I went out to relieve myself in the forest, it looked as if there was a fire blazing underneath the big tree in front of Rinpoche's retreat hut. Once I told Apo Shedrup about it, but he said nothing. Sometimes there seemed to be small fires alight everywhere, and sometimes there seemed to be fire inside the hut. Finally, I asked Rinpoche about the fire. He said that it was the protector Rahula, and told me not to go near it.

"Rinpoche would never lie down at night; he slept sitting up straight in his wooden box. In the evening, after supper, he would start his meditation session and not speak until lunchtime the next day. At lunchtime his brother would call me and we would all have lunch together, and talk a little. Then, right away, Rinpoche would start another session and not see anyone until evening.

"At White Grove, where Rinpoche spent three years in retreat, he also received the reading transmission for the *Tripitaka*, the 103 volumes of the Buddhist Canon. That was after our first daughter, Chimé, was born. Rinpoche's room was so small that there was nowhere inside where the lama reading the texts could sit. So a place for him was arranged outside on the veranda, among the flowerpots, and he read through the window. Rinpoche's mother, his brother Shedrup, and I also received the transmission, but because Rinpoche was still in

The mandala of the Buddha of Eternal Life, Amitayus, as it arose in Khyentse Rinpoche's mind:

"Once, I stayed near a sacred lake at the foot of the snow peaks of Ri Gangkar, praying fervently for the long life of my teacher, Khyentse Chökyi Lodrö. As I was offering a sacred feast based on Amitayus, the outline of the mandala appeared clearly on the surface of the lake. The text of the Lotus Essence of Life then arose in my mind and I wrote it down."

Mandalas are objects of meditation whose purpose is to transform and purify our ordinary perception of the world: to lead us to the recognition that the Buddha-nature is present in every sentient being, just as oil pervades every sesame seed, and to see primordial purity and perfection in all phenomena.

We visualize ourselves as the central deity, not a "god" but a manifestation of our own pure nature.

The palace in which the deity dwells is made of various jewels symbolizing the Buddhas' wisdom, compassion, and activity arising as forms and colors to fulfill beings' aspirations. Its square shape indicates that the absolute nature is without distortion. Its four doors symbolize the four boundless qualities: love, compassion, joy, and impartiality. The five different colored layers of its walls symbolize the five wisdoms, which are the purified aspects of the five poisons (ignorance, hatred, desire, pride, and jealousy). Made of light, the palace has neither outside nor inside, symbolizing that phenomena are the display of primordial wisdom. The fire of wisdom encircling the whole mandala indicates that ignorance and all the other obscurations of the mind have been burned up for ever.

retreat nobody else came. During the transmission Rinpoche used to do his sessions just as before.

"Even after his retreat, Rinpoche would only stay at the family house for a week or two at a time before returning to his hermitage.

"One of Rinpoche's nephews was often out hunting, and had a gun that was famous for its accuracy. One day, when Rinpoche visited their house, his mother—Rinpoche's sister—told him: 'This gun has killed so many animals; please bless it.' Rinpoche put the gun to his mouth and blew into it. It never fired again. After that, whenever Rinpoche was invited to visit any of the rich herdsmen who were fond of hunting, they would hide all their guns.

"Rinpoche had a relative called Apo Jamtse, who had a huge mastiff that used to chase and kill sheep and goats belonging to the poor people around. None of them dared to punish a dog that belonged to the powerful Dilgo family. One day when Rinpoche went to have tea with Apo Jamtse's family, Rinpoche's aunt, Ashi Kaga, who ran the household, told him about the dog and asked what they should do about it. At that moment, Rinpoche was eating a ball of roasted barley. He blew on it, and threw it to the dog. The dog ate it up, and after that never attacked animals again. The poor people around were very happy.

"A master called Drungnam Gyatrul exchanged many teachings with Khyentse Rinpoche. He spent his whole life at Ngoma Nangsum, in a cave in a rock shaped like a *vajra* and surrounded by meadows. He hardly ever slept. Five or six hundred of his disciples lived in nearby caves and practised the mantra of Guru Padmasambhava. He lived in a cave in the very middle of the rock, which had been circumambulated by so many people that the earth had been worn away down to waist level. We stayed in a tent nearby, and Rinpoche would spend all day in the cave with Gyatrul Rinpoche receiving teachings from him. During that month, Gyatrul Rinpoche and I were the only people who saw him.

"Our younger daughter was a very special child. I gave birth to her in a tent in a forest clearing above Cliff Hermitage. It was after dark when she was born, but shortly afterwards there was a light as bright as daylight. I wondered what that light could be. It rained heavily, and the light continued until two or three in the morning. When Rinpoche was told about this light he did not seem to pay much attention. The girl's mind was very special. She was so virtuous and devoted to the Buddhist teachings, and she loved to practice. All the servants were very fond of her. She died in India soon after we escaped from Tibet."

After completing his retreat at the age of twenty-eight, Khyentse Rinpoche spent many years with Dzongsar Khyentse Chökyi Lodrö (1896–1959), who was, like him, an incarnation of the first Khyentse. Khyentse Rinpoche considered Chökyi Lodrö his second main teacher and had immense respect for him. After receiving the six-month empowerments of the *Collection of Revealed Treasures* from Chökyi Lodrö, Khyentse Rinpoche told him that he wished to spend the rest of his life in solitary meditation. But Khyentse Chökyi Lodrö was adamant. "Your mind and mine are one," he said. "The time has come for you to teach and transmit to others the countless precious teachings you have received." So from then on, Khyentse Rinpoche worked constantly for the benefit of all living beings with the tireless energy that is the hallmark of the Khyentse lineage. He tells of the times he spent at Dzongsar:

"When I arrived for the first time, Khyentse Chökyi Lodrö Rinpoche told me that the night before he had dreamt of meeting the first Khyentse, Jamyang Khyentse Wangpo. 'It is a very auspicious sign that you have come today,' he said.

"On my first visit to Dzongsar, I stayed for only two months. Gradually I began to go there every summer, returning to Denkhok for the winter or visiting other places to receive teachings from many different masters.

"For me, returning to Dzongsar was always a great event, to which I looked forward eagerly. I was always lodged in Khyentse Chökyi Lodrö's quarters. Most of the time we would take our meals together so that we could talk to each other. When people came to see him, I would go to a next-door room and practice there until he was free again, whereupon we would resume our conversation. While many of Dzongsar's ordinary monks were not conspicuously enthusiastic about study and practice, and approached their duties as a routine, the monastery's college students studied hard and usually enjoyed easy access to Chökyi Lodrö, who took great pleasure in being with them. But when I was there I heard them groaning that now he would have no time to see them.

"When I left he would accompany me right up to the door of his residence. He was always reluctant to let me leave, and on many occasions I could see tears in his eyes.

"Khyentse Chökyi Lodrö was also a finder of concealed treasures, and once he told me: 'You must find many treasures with which to benefit others. I had a dream last night. There were clouds in the shapes of the eight auspicious symbols and many other forms, and with them in the sky were many Buddhas and Bodhisattvas. From those clouds fell an abundant rain of nectar, benefiting beings. You must spread your treasure teachings.' He asked me to give him the empowerments for some of my treasures, and I offered them to him."

Khyentse Chökyi Lodrö asked Khyentse Rinpoche to go to Amdo province and teach the *Treasury of Rediscovered Teachings*. Here is Rinpoche's wife's account of that journey:

"Rinpoche traveled to Rekong, in Amdo, near Lake Kokonor. One very cold day, some herdsmen invited Rinpoche to their tent and offered him and his party a large quantity of butter, dried meat, and sweet cheese for the journey. Rinpoche—unusually—warned one of his attendants to look after the horses carefully. When the time came to leave, the attendant rushed in, exclaiming that

Khyentse Rinpoche surrounded by some of the yogis of Rekong, in the province of Amdo, in the 1950s (see text). *The yogis wear their matted hair, in some cases up to five feet long, wound around their heads. Khyentse Rinpoche's two daughters are seated to his left.*

the horses had disappeared; he had left them for a while and they must have been stolen. Fortunately, the herdsmen had many yaks and gave some to Rinpoche, who reached Rekong after a month's journey.

"In Rekong, Rinpoche gave the empowerments of the *Treasury of Rediscovered Teachings* over four months to 1,900 yogis. When Rinpoche's hosts heard from his monks about the robbery of his horses, they were quite upset; but Rinpoche told them that he had arrived safely and so it was now of no concern. However, some of the Rekong yogis, known for their magic power, said that they could not just leave the matter like that. Two weeks after Rinpoche started teaching, the robbers arrived with all the stolen horses and begged Rinpoche to take them back. Rinpoche replied that he no longer needed the horses and they could keep them, but the robbers refused to listen. After the theft of the horses, they said, everything had gone wrong for them. When they milked their cows they got not milk but blood. One boy had been attacked by vultures—something quite unheard of—and many of the clan had fallen ill. Finally, they just left the horses near the monastery and rode away.

"Rinpoche stayed at Rekong Monastery for a year, and gave teachings at a beautiful hilltop site where the famous nineteenth-century yogi Shabkar Tsogdruk Rangdrol had lived. There was a large rock, with a tree behind it, on which Shabkar used to sit and sing his famous spiritual songs. The local people offered this seat to Rinpoche, and when he improvised songs there, rainbows appeared and snowflakes fell gently, like flowers. Everyone said that he must be a reincarnation of Shabkar.

"Rinpoche had an attendant, a ritual master called Achog, whom he often had to reprimand. One night Achog ran away, leaving a piece of cloth as an offering and a note saying that he felt unable to serve Rinpoche properly and had therefore decided to leave. After walking for a month he reached a nomad herdsman's camp in Golok, and in one of the black yak-hair tents a mother and daughter asked him to perform some ceremonies for them in exchange for food and lodging. It was freezing cold and he had nowhere else to go, so he agreed. By then he had fallen quite ill.

"One day the mother called out to Achog that a stranger, a tall lama on a big horse, was approaching the tent. Achog looked through the door and saw Khyentse Rinpoche with an attendant riding straight up to the tent. Rinpoche dismounted, came in, and asked: 'Achog, how are you?' Achog was so astounded that he began to cry. Rinpoche told him there was no need to cry and that he had better come back with them. The old mother offered Rinpoche tea, milk, and curd. In answer to Achog's questions, Rinpoche's attendant said that no one had told them where to find him, nor had they met anyone in the snow-covered landscape to give them directions to the camp. Rinpoche said it was time to go, and all three came back home together. In those days, people used to say that Rinpoche had incredible clairvoyance."

In order to conquer the high ground of the uncreated nature of mind, we must go to the source and recognize the origin of our thoughts. Otherwise, one thought gives rise to a second thought, the second thought to a third, and so on forever. We are constantly assailed by memories of the past and carried away by expectations for the future, and lose all awareness of the present.

It is our own mind that leads us astray into the cycle of existences. Blind to the mind's true nature, we hold fast to our thoughts, which are nothing but manifestations of that nature. This freezes awareness into solid concepts, such as I and other, desirable and detestable, and plenty of others. This is how we create samsara.

But if, instead of letting our thoughts solidify, we recognize their emptiness, then each thought that arises and disappears in the mind renders the realization of emptiness ever clearer.

In the heart of winter, the chill freezes lakes and rivers; water becomes so solid that it can bear men, beasts, and carts. As spring approaches, earth and water warm up and thaw. What then remains of the hardness of the ice? Water is soft and fluid, ice hard and sharp, so we cannot say that they are identical; but neither can we say that they are different, because ice is only solidified water, and water is only melted ice.

The same applies to our perception of the world around us. To be attached to the reality of phenomena, to be tormented by attraction and repulsion, by pleasure and pain, gain and loss, fame and obscurity, praise and blame, creates a solidity in the mind. What we have to do, therefore, is to melt the ice of concepts into the living water of the freedom within.

All phenomena of samsara and nirvana arise like a rainbow, and like a rainbow they are devoid of any tangible existence. Once you have recognized the true nature of reality, which is empty and at the same time appears as the phenomenal world, your mind will cease to be under the power of delusion. If you know how to leave your thoughts free to dissolve by themselves as they arise, they will cross your mind as a bird crosses the sky—without leaving any trace.

Maintain that state of simplicity. If you encounter happiness, success, prosperity, or other favorable conditions, consider them as dreams and illusions, and do not get attached to them. If you are stricken by illness, calumny, deprivation, or other physical and mental trials, do not let yourself get discouraged, but rekindle your compassion and generate the wish that through your suffering all beings' sufferings may be exhausted. Whatever circumstances arise, do not plunge into either elation or misery, but stay free and comfortable, in unshakable serenity.

Khyentse Rinpoche

THE CIRCLE OF TRANSFORMATION

A beautiful country is a dreamlike illusion,
It's senseless to cling to it.
Unless the inner forces of negative emotions
    are conquered,
Strife with outer enemies will never end.

Khyentse Rinpoche

By the late 1950s, the Chinese takeover of Tibet, which had been proceeding by slow infiltration for the previous decade, was rapidly turning into a full-scale military invasion—particularly in Kham, in the east. When Chinese officials came to Denkhok and inquired about Khyentse Rinpoche's whereabouts, his wife sent him a secret message warning him not to come home. She urged him to go from Khampagar, a monastery he was then visiting, straight to Lhasa. She herself narrowly escaped the ubiquitous Chinese soldiers to join him on the road. They hurried to Lhasa, leaving everything behind, including Rinpoche's precious books and most of his writings. The rest of the family soon joined him. Together, they went on a pilgrimage in Central Tibet. Then, for six months, Khyentse Rinpoche sat before the famous Crowned Buddha statue in Lhasa to recite one hundred thousand offerings of the mandala of the universe. An epidemic was raging in Lhasa, so he also performed many ceremonies and prayers for the sick and dying, turning a deaf ear to his family's fears that he himself would be infected. During the epidemic, his mother and his elder brother, Shedrup, both died.

By then, the news had come that the Chinese had confiscated the Dilgo family estate in Kham and taken all their possessions. Rinpoche's wife, Khandro Lhamo, recounts:

“One day in Lhasa some Chinese officials came to see me and asked: 'Revered consort, what are you doing?'

Khyentse Rinpoche in Kalimpong, India, in 1959, shortly after escaping from Tibet.

“I replied that I had just been sitting there, and offered them some fruit. They asked what my daughters were doing and I said that they were doing prostrations at Lhasa's main temple. They asked me if I missed my home and if Rinpoche and I were planning to go back. I said we did miss our home, and wanted to return soon. Then they asked why we had come to Central Tibet, and whether Communism had already been established in Kham at the time we had left. I answered that we had come on pilgrimage—and as for Communism, it was a word I had never heard before. The Chinese, seeing some red and white sweets laid out on the table, asked if it was our custom to eat red and white sweets. When I answered yes, they said that Communism was just like red and white sweets. I asked them what the purpose of Communism was, and they said that it was something very good, just like the sweets. I told them that if it was anything like those sweets I had a good chance of finding it to my liking.

“By then I knew that the Chinese had seized all our possessions and horses in Eastern Tibet, but I pretended to know nothing. I was afraid that they might arrest us. They told me to be ready to travel back to Kham, where we would get Chinese ranks; Rinpoche would be paid a thousand yuan, and I would be paid five hundred. I thanked them very much and said we would be ready to go.

“Everyone from Kham who had come to Lhasa was being arrested and taken back. Some were forced to leave their children behind, and were devastated. Some jumped into the water to escape or to take their own lives, but most of them were tied up and put in trucks. So I immediately went to join Rinpoche at Tsurphu, the seat of the Karmapa, to the northwest of Lhasa. We now had no choice but to escape. We had left our horses grazing near Tsurphu, but the Chinese had stolen them all. So I borrowed a horse, rode to Lhasa, and bought twelve more horses. I set back out that night and arrived at dawn. Pawo Rinpoche also gave us a very strong horse. Yaks carried our luggage. Rinpoche always walked. It is hard to compare Rinpoche with other lamas; he was very humble and used to look after everyone. There were thirteen of us. We walked for about a month and a half, pitching tents at night.

"When we were only a few days' journey from the Bhutanese border, we learned that the Chinese troops were closing in on us from behind. So we had no choice but to abandon all our luggage, mostly books and precious statues, in order to travel unnoticed and faster, and took to hiding during the day and walking at night. Many Tibetans were fleeing, and the Chinese were shooting on sight. We climbed a mountain pass and were so exhausted that we stayed the night there. It was bitterly cold. Rinpoche sat on a rock, Nyenpa Rinpoche on the other side. I sat nearby. All the yaks were still saddled; we had nothing to feed them with. It snowed for three days and nights. We couldn't make a fire to boil tea, as the Chinese would see the smoke. There was nowhere to go, just endless rock screes.

"When finally we reached the Bhutanese border, we had hardly anything left to eat—just a tiny bit of barley flour, butter, and dry meat. For twelve days we had to wait on a high mountain on the border while the Bhutanese soldiers awaited their instructions. Finally, the Bhutanese government allowed us to enter. They were very kind to us and gave everyone barley and rice. An old lady gave us each some soup. We went through the forests of Bhutan in constant rain, and there were so many leeches that both humans and horses were bleeding everywhere.

"When we reached a place called Wangdi, someone heard the news on a small radio that Khyentse Chökyi Lodrö had died in Sikkim.

"When we reached India, I was very surprised to see all the cars and the trains. By then Khyentse Rinpoche was forty-nine. He went to perform the cremation of Khyentse Chökyi Lodrö in Sikkim. In Kalimpong and Darjeeling he also met other great lamas such as Dudjom Rinpoche and Kangyur Rinpoche, with whom he exchanged teachings."

At the request of the Bhutanese royal family, Khyentse Rinpoche went to live in Bhutan. He became a schoolteacher near Thimphu, the capital. Soon his inner perfection drew many disciples to him and, as the years passed, he became the foremost Buddhist teacher in Bhutan, revered by all from the king down to the humblest farmer.

One evening, in Paro, he suddenly asked one of his monks to go to the capital Thimphu, two hours' drive away, to take a small image of the protectress Ekajati to the young king, with a message that the king should keep it on his body the next day. The next morning, as the king drove down toward the Indian border, his jeep, missing a turning on the mountain road, fell over the precipitous edge, rebounding several times before crashing far below. Everyone was killed except the king, who found himself ejected from the car as it fell, and was unharmed. Other similar events strongly confirmed the faith and confidence people felt in Khyentse Rinpoche.

Bhutan is a mountain kingdom that has managed to remain unconquered and independent ever since Vajrayana Buddhism was first introduced—in the eighth century by Guru Padmasambhava, and then by the fifteenth-century Bhutanese *tertön* Pema Lingpa and the influential seventeenth-century Tibetan teacher Shabdrung Ngawang Namgyal. Buddhist culture has been able to flourish unimpeded, and its values are deeply embedded in people's minds. Every hill is topped by a small temple, surrounded by prayer flags flapping in the wind. Prayer wheels are kept in motion day and night by torrents and rivulets. Mountain and forest are dotted with hermitages in which retreatants devote their time to meditation. They come down into the valleys once a year, at harvesttime, to beg for alms, and at every farm they are given a measure of rice and dry vegetables. Within a month they receive enough provisions to stay the rest of the year in solitary retreat.

Wherever Khyentse Rinpoche went in Bhutan, every morning long before dawn devotees would start queuing at his door, waiting for him to finish his morning prayers. At last they would go in to offer him rice flakes, roasted barley flour, cottage cheese, and fresh butter heaped in round, finely woven baskets of multicolored straw. They would ask him for his prayers for their well-being, and he would put his hand on their heads in blessing.

When Khyentse Rinpoche traveled in Bhutan, it seemed that the whole country knew about it. Every ten miles or so, near a farm or a village, a group

(continued on page 70)

Khyentse Rinpoche with his wife and two daughters photographed in Lhasa, Tibet, in 1957.

Towering mountain clad in virgin forests,
Your peak, majestic in its snowy turban,
    stretches to the skies,
Your chest is draped with silvery scarves of mist:
How happy the carefree yogis who let go
    of this life's affairs!

Khyentse Rinpoche

When you see a lofty mountain
Be reminded of the inner view:
The view is the teacher's mind,
Inseparable from the nature of your own.

When you see a lovely forest,
Be reminded of experiences and realization:
Have no hopes or doubts about them,
They are all the teacher's play.

When you see a garden of flowers
Be reminded of action, naturally free:
All actions in harmony with Dharma
Are the teacher's perfect life.

However deluded your thoughts may be,
They are but products of your intellect.
If you set your thoughts free
Where nothing arises, remains, or ends,
They will vanish into emptiness.
That naked emptiness is the guru:
Primordial wisdom beyond the intellect.

Khyentse Rinpoche

Space, whose nature is free of concepts,
Encompasses everything;
Likewise, the stainless expanse of the mind's true nature
Permeates all beings.

Maitreya-Asanga

(left) *Paro Taktsang, the "Tiger's Nest" in Bhutan, one of the sites most sacred to Guru Padmasambhava, who is said to have flown there riding a tigress. Many of his "spiritual treasures" were concealed there. The temples were built on the vertiginous cliff in the seventeenth century.*

(right) *Khyentse Rinpoche spent several weeks at Paro Taktsang in 1980, making offerings of one hundred thousand butter lamps and giving teachings and empowerments (see page 70). In this photograph he is seen gazing at the landscape from a balcony projecting over the sheer precipice during a ceremony to revitalize the blessings of this sacred place.*

Beside a plunging waterfall near the entrance to the "Tiger's Nest" of Paro Taktsang (previous pages) an aged nun lives in this small retreat hermitage, the only access to which is a series of notched tree-trunks leaning precariously against the sheer rock face.

Some of the many monks who accompanied Khyentse Rinpoche during his visit to Paro Taktsang in 1980, playing twelve-foot-long Tibetan trumpets on one of the site's terraces. The forests of the Paro Valley stretch out below.

W hat we normally call the mind is the deluded mind, a turbulent vortex of thoughts whipped up by attachment, anger, and ignorance. This mind, unlike enlightened awareness, is always being carried away by one delusion after another. Thoughts of hatred or attachment suddenly arise without warning, triggered off by such circumstances as an unexpected meeting with an adversary or a friend, and unless they are immediately overpowered with the proper antidote they quickly take root and proliferate, reinforcing the habitual predominance of hatred or attachment in the mind and adding more and more karmic imprints.

Yet, however strong these thoughts may seem, they are just thoughts and will eventually dissolve back into emptiness. Once you recognize the intrinsic nature of the mind, these thoughts that seem to appear and disappear all the time can no longer fool you. Just as clouds form, last for a while, and then dissolve back into the empty sky, so deluded thoughts arise, remain for a while, and then vanish in the emptiness of mind; in reality nothing at all has happened.

When sunlight falls on a crystal, lights of all colors of the rainbow appear; yet they have no substance that you can grasp. Likewise, all thoughts in their infinite variety—devotion, compassion, harmfulness, desire— are utterly without substance. This is the mind of the Buddha. There is no thought that is something other than voidness; if you recognize the void nature of thoughts at the very moment they arise, they will dissolve. Attachment and hatred will never be able to disturb the mind. Deluded emotions will collapse by themselves. No negative actions will be accumulated, so no suffering will follow.

Khyentse Rinpoche

(opposite) *The massive monastery-fortress of Tashicho Dzong in Thimphu, capital of Bhutan. One half of the building is occupied by over a thousand monks, and the other half by different departments of the government and of the king's office. The capital is situated in a steep-sided valley at an altitude of six thousand feet.*

If a man has compassion, he is Buddha;
Without compassion, he is Lord of Death.

With compassion, the root of Dharma is planted,
Without compassion, the root of Dharma is rotten.

One with compassion is kind even when angry,
One without compassion kills even as he smiles.

For one with compassion, even enemies turn into friends,
Without compassion, even friends turn into enemies.

With compassion, one has all Dharmas,
Without compassion, one has no Dharma at all.

With compassion, one is a true Buddhist,
Without compassion, one is worse than profane.

Even meditating on voidness, one needs compassion as its essence.
A Dharma practitioner must have a compassionate nature.

Great compassion is like a wish-fulfilling gem.
Great compassion fulfills the hopes of self and others.

Therefore, all of you, renunciants and householders,
Cultivate compassion and you will achieve Buddhahood.
Shabkar

*Monks dressed as two of the sixteen offering goddesses, with golden crowns and bone
ornaments, each holding a bell and a* vajra, *for a long ritual, or* drupchen, *lasting nine
continuous days and nights. Every morning, as the assembly chants an offering prayer,
the sixteen goddesses slowly circle the mandala making gestures* (mudra) *that symbolize
the offering of flowers, incense, lamps, perfume, and so forth.*

Khyentse Rinpoche performing a fire ceremony (chinsek), *an offering ritual during which precious substances are offered to the deities of the mandala visualized in the fire. There are four kinds of fire offering, corresponding to the four kinds of enlightened activity; for each of them a different color is used for the ritual implements and substances, the costumes, and the wood burned in the fire. Here, the ritual is intended to* attract *favorable circumstances, and the predominant color is red; on other occasions it might be to* pacify *disease, wars, and negative emotions, in which case the color would be white; to* increase *merit, life span, and meditational experiences, the color would be yellow; or to* subjugate *inner and outer obstacles and negative forces, the color would be dark blue. The setting here is the courtyard of the seventh-century temple of Paro Kyichu in Western Bhutan.*

*A Bhutanese monk plays a
drum to accompany the ritual
music for a ceremony.*

Just as no darkness exists at the center of the sun,
To a yogi, universe and beings all arise as deities—
And the yogi is content.

Just as no ordinary stones exist on an island of gold,
To a yogi all sounds resound as mantras—
And the yogi is content.

Just as a bird crossing a clear, empty sky leaves no trace,
To a yogi all thoughts arise as the absolute—
And the yogi is content.

In the vastness of awareness not confined to formal sessions,
To a yogi all meditation is relaxed and at ease—
And the yogi is content.

Free from the workings of mind,
I realize that phenomena are the absolute state.
You, my friend, should realize this too.
Don't trust intellectual teachings—
Recognize that vast and unborn sameness.

Shabkar

*Khyentse Rinpoche's grandson, Rabjam Rinpoche, officiates
in the late-night concluding ceremony of a week-long ritual for
dispelling obstacles and ensuring peace.*

(above) *A clown takes part in a sacred dance festival in Thimphu, both to entertain the spectators and to keep the crowd clear of the dancing area.*

(right) *During a sacred dance performance, this seated figure represents a hunter at the moment of death, face-to-face with the consequences of his negative actions. In the drama he is being judged by the fearsome figure of the Lord of Death, a symbolic personification of the immutable law of cause and effect by which positive and negative actions are bound to result in happiness and suffering.*

If you vanquish ego-clinging today, tonight you will be enlightened. If you vanquish it tomorrow, you will be enlightened tomorrow night. But if you never vanquish it, you will never be enlightened. Yet "I" is just a thought. Thoughts and feelings have no intrinsic solidity, form, shape, or color. When a thought of anger arises in the mind with such force that you feel aggressive and destructive, is anger brandishing a weapon? Is it at the head of an army? Can it burn things like fire, crush them like a rock, or carry them away like a violent river? No. Anger, like any other thought or feeling, has no true existence—not even a definite location in your body, speech, or mind. It is just like wind roaring in empty space.

Instead of allowing wild thoughts to enslave you, realize their essential emptiness. If you subdue the hatred within, you will discover that there is not a single enemy left outside. Otherwise, even if you could overpower everyone in the whole world, your hatred would only grow stronger. Indulging it will never make it subside. The only truly intolerable enemy is hatred itself. Examine the nature of hatred; you will find that it is no more than a thought. When you see it as it is, it will dissolve like a cloud in the sky.

Khyentse Rinpoche

Kuje Lhakhang in Bumthang, Eastern Bhutan. In 1983 Khyentse Rinpoche gave the "reading transmission" of the 103 volumes of the entire Buddhist Canon, the words of the Buddha. On the first day, the volumes of the scriptures, from which he will be reading all day long for the next three months to several thousand disciples, are carried in procession to the tent erected in front of the monastery.

You and all beings are equal in wanting to be happy;
You and all beings are equal in wanting not to suffer.

In order to get used to caring for others more than yourself,
You should visualize the exchange of yourself and others:
As you breathe in and out,
Take their suffering upon yourself and send them
     your happiness.

Realize that whatever arises is the display of the absolute,
The primordial nature, unbroken simplicity.
If you don't cling, whatever arises is naturally freed.
Simply remain in the great equal taste, without rejecting
     or accepting.

Childish sentient beings, not knowing this,
Treat phenomena as if they were solid and real;
Thus begins a chain of attractions and aversions,
And the great sufferings of existence—a nonexistent
     masquerade!

The powerful roots are
Ignorance and taking beings and phenomena to exist truly;
Conditioned existence comes about
From getting used to those things.

Nothing to illuminate,
Nothing to eliminate,
Looking perfectly at perfection itself,
Seeing perfection, one is perfectly free.

Shechen Gyaltsap

A thick forest of prayer flags, as found everywhere in Bhutan—on hilltops, in forest clearings, on top of rocky out-crops, at river confluences, and near temples. They are replaced once or twice a year by local people, who print them from wooden blocks, take them to a lama to be consecrated, and fix them to bamboo poles (see page 10).

(above) *The monastery of Punakha, situated between two rivers, the Phochu and the Mochu, at their confluence in Central Bhutan. The monastery serves as the winter quarters of the thousand monks of Thimphu Dzong* (see page 52), *who used to make the three-day journey on foot.*
(opposite) *In the courtyard of Punakha Monastery, during a nine-day* drupchen *ceremony led by Khyentse Rinpoche, the monks perform a ritual with musical instruments to recon- secrate the ground.*

All the joy the world contains
Has come through wishing happiness for others.
All the misery the world contains
Has come through wanting pleasure for oneself.

Is there need for lengthy explanation?
Childish beings look out for themselves.
Buddhas labor for the good of others:
See the difference that divides them!

Bringing joy to beings, then, I please the Buddhas also—
Offending them, the Buddhas I offend.

Shantideva

(above) *A hermit, who spends most of his time in solitary retreat, paints a mandala diagram (see page 42) for the use of a fellow practitioner.*
(right) *A calligrapher copies a sacred text onto handmade paper held in his left hand. The art of calligraphy is still very much alive in Bhutan, and a skilled calligrapher can copy up to fifteen pages a day. He uses a pen of sharpened bamboo and ink made from the thick soot of the kitchen hearth, finely ground and mixed with water and a natural glue.*

Like the earth and the pervading elements,
Enduring like the sky itself endures,
For boundless multitudes of living beings,
May I be their ground and sustenance.

Thus for everything that lives,
As far as are the limits of the sky,
May I provide their livelihood and nourishment
Until they pass beyond the bonds of suffering.

For all those ailing in the world,
Until their every sickness has been healed,
May I myself become for them
The doctor, nurse, the medicine itself.

Raining down a flood of food and drink,
May I dispel the ills of thirst and famine.
And in the ages marked by scarcity and want,
May I myself appear as drink and sustenance.

For sentient beings, poor and destitute,
May I become a treasure ever-plentiful,
And lie before them closely in their reach,
A varied source of all that they might need.

My body, thus, and all my goods besides,
And all my merits gained and to be gained,
I give them all away withholding nothing
To bring about the benefit of beings.

Shantideva

Shechen Rabjam Rinpoche performs a fire ceremony, similar to the one described on page 55.

67

(above) *Four characteristically sturdy monks from Kham, in Eastern Tibet, who have come to receive teachings from Khyentse Rinpoche in Kuje Lhakhang in Bumthang, in Eastern Bhutan.*

All four have completed at least five or six years of retreat in Tibet. The one on the left has recited the mantra of Guru Pad-masambhava one hundred million times.

(opposite) *Khyentse Rinpoche performs a ritual by torchlight before dawn on the last day of a long ceremony in Punakha. The mandala that has been the focal point of the ceremony will be dis-mantled, and from each of its component elements the partici-pants will symbolically receive the power and blessings gathered throughout the ceremony by their meditations.*

(continued from page 47)

of people, sometimes with a few monks, would be waiting by the roadside. A big fire piled with moist juniper branches would send billows of fragrant smoke to the sky. Some handwoven woollen carpets would be spread out in front of a wooden table, beautifully carved with dragons, birds, and lotus flowers, bearing delicacies and pots of hot tea. The party would stop and be offered refreshments. Sometimes Khyentse Rinpoche would give his blessings from the car, sometimes he would get out and sit for a while to give a longevity blessing to the assembled crowd.

When reaching a larger monastery or village, Khyentse Rinpoche would be awaited by a long procession of monks and local dignitaries. Led by monks playing music and holding aloft their brocade banners, sometimes dancing, a slow procession would take him to his quarters. There, the mayor, chief justice, and other notables, in ceremonial dress with a sword in its silver scabbard at their waists, would prostrate themselves before him and offer him tea and food. The next day, thousands of people would gather from all around in the courtyard of the monastery, and Khyentse Rinpoche would give them his blessings as they filed past him for hours. When the crowd was too large, he would be carried on a litter between the seated rows of devotees in an open field, scattering consecrated rice among them.

Having reached his destination, Khyentse Rinpoche would usually stay for a month or more, giving teachings and performing major ceremonies. As soon as these were completed, he would move on. He traveled throughout the year, taking with him a dozen big bundles of books and ritual objects. He would be accompanied by five or six monk attendants and by a following of incarnate lamas and practitioners, who would receive regular teachings from him for one or two hours every day, wherever they were.

Three or four times a year, Khyentse Rinpoche would perform large ceremonies called *drupchen*, or great accomplishments, lasting from eight to fourteen continuous days and nights. The whole congregation gathered from seven in the morning until seven in the evening, and during the night would be divided into three groups that took turns to maintain the flow of the ritual and of the uninterrupted recitation of mantras. These ceremonies, in beautiful temples surrounded by fields and forests, would be punctuated with sacred music, dance, and symbolic offering gestures and rituals.

Once Khyentse Rinpoche spent two weeks at the Tiger's Nest Cave at Paro Taktsang. There he made offerings of one hundred thousand butter lamps and gave many teachings and empowerments. While he was there, he had a vision of the great eighteenth-century lama Jigme Lingpa, who had a book on his head, tied up in his hair, and wore a white robe and a red-and-white striped shawl. He put his hand on Khyentse Rinpoche's head and told him: "You are the heir of my teachings, the Heart Essence of Vast Space (*Longchen Nyingthig*). You may do with them whatever you wish." Jigme Lingpa also told him that to maintain

Dharamsala, India, 1991. His Holiness the Dalai Lama offers a symbolic representation of the universe to Khyentse Rinpoche at the beginning of a teaching he has requested.

peace in Bhutan and to ensure the preservation of the Buddhist teachings, four large stupas should be built. Each stupa should contain one hundred thousand miniature clay stupas. This was done accordingly.

Khyentse Rinpoche was one of those rare teachers with a special capacity who are known in the Nyingma tradition as *tertön*, discoverers of spiritual treasures, meaning that they are able to reveal teachings concealed by Guru Padmasambhava for the sake of future generations. When the lotus-born guru, Padmasambhava, gave ripening empowerments and liberating instructions to King Trisong Detsen, to the *dakini* Yeshe Tsogyal, and to the other twenty-five main disciples, he entrusted special teachings to each of them and miraculously concealed these as "treasures" in various places—temple buildings, sacred images, rocks, lakes, and even the sky. He prophesied that these particular disciples would be reborn in the future and take these teachings out of their place of concealment, using and transmitting them for the sake of the beings of their time. When the right time comes, a *tertön* experiences visions or signs indicating how and where to discover his or her destined treasure, or *terma*. In the case of so-called "mind treasures," the teachings are not physically unearthed but arise in the *tertön*'s mind, and this was the chosen method for most of those revealed by Khyentse Rinpoche. Over the centuries, a few hundred *tertön* masters have appeared. This mode of transmission, sometimes termed the "short" lineage, complements the "long" lineage of the canonical scriptures, transmitted from master to disciple over the generations since Padmasambhava's time.

In one of these *terma* visions, Khyentse Rinpoche saw the complete mandala of the Buddha of eternal life (see page 42) appear on the surface of a lake in Eastern Tibet. Following this vision, he wrote a whole volume of teachings and spiritual practices. Altogether, Khyentse Rinpoche's spiritual treasures fill five volumes.

After escaping from Tibet and arriving in India, Khyentse Rinpoche became one of the main teachers of His Holiness the Dalai Lama. As he recounts in his autobiography, he first met the Dalai Lama in Lhasa:

"Once I was saying prayers in the Jokhang Temple in Lhasa, near the new statue of Guru Padmasambhava. Suddenly I smelled some very fragrant incense, and some brocade-clad officials came in followed by a pale-faced monk wearing glasses. He looked like the pictures I had seen of His Holiness the Dalai Lama. He was examining the new statue of Guru Padmasambhava, and offered a ceremonial scarf before it. When he passed near me, he asked where I was from, what was my name, and what ceremony I was performing. He told me to say my prayers well, and went to the Crowned Buddha temple, where he stayed for about an hour. That was my first meeting with His Holiness.

"I met him again later on two occasions at his summer residence in Lhasa with my brother Sangye Nyenpa Rinpoche.

"After we finally reached India, Nyenpa Rinpoche was on pilgrimage in Varanasi and met the Dalai Lama there. His Holiness asked where his tall brother with long hair was, and if he had been harmed by the Chinese. He was pleased to know that we had escaped safely and said that we would meet later."

Not long afterward, all the main lamas of the four schools of Tibetan Buddhism gathered in Dharamsala, the Dalai Lama's seat in India, to offer prayers for his long life and discuss the preservation of the Tibetan Buddhist teachings in exile. The Nyingma, Sakya, and Kagyu schools were asked to choose a representative to offer the Dalai Lama a mandala symbolizing the whole universe. On such occasions, whoever makes the offering traditionally starts by delivering a long, erudite speech describing the universe according to Buddhist cosmology and the fundamental tenets of Buddhist history and doctrine. Usually, a great scholar would compose such a discourse over a few weeks and read

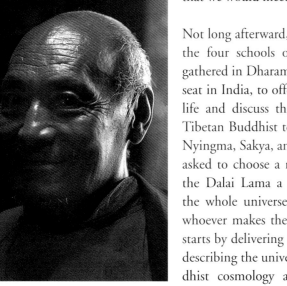

Kangyur Rinpoche (1898–1975), a master who was both Khyentse Rinpoche's teacher and his disciple.

Khyentse Rinpoche with Dudjom Rinpoche (1904–1987), then head of the Nyingma tradition, in the Dordogne, France, 1984.

it out on the day, but Khyentse Rinpoche was asked to give the discourse only the day before. Nevertheless, he accepted without much formality. A scholar heard what had happened and felt sorry that Khyentse Rinpoche had been asked to give such an important lecture without preparation. He brought him a book containing the text of a similar lecture, and suggested that Khyentse Rinpoche might study it or read from it the next day. Khyentse Rinpoche thanked the scholar politely, but put the book down on his table, resumed the conversation he had been having with his visitors, and then went to sleep.

The next day, when the time came to give the lecture in the presence of the Dalai Lama and the learned assembly, Khyentse Rinpoche stood up, opened the book for the first time, and holding it—without turning the pages—delivered a highly erudite discourse lasting some two hours. At the end, during the offering of the Eight Auspicious Objects to the Dalai Lama, a clap of thunder was heard as he took the conch shell in his hands.

Everyone was struck by Khyentse Rinpoche's learning, which thereafter was well-known among the Tibetan community in India. The next day, as Khyentse Rinpoche was saying good-bye to him, the Dalai Lama said: "That was an auspicious sign yesterday with the thunder, was it not?"

Later he asked Khyentse Rinpoche to his residence in Dharamsala many times. Over the years, Khyentse Rinpoche offered him most of the major teachings from the Nyingma tradition.

His Holiness the Dalai Lama, spiritual and temporal leader of Tibet, giving the empowerment of Kalachakra, the Wheel of Time, in Bodhgaya, India, 1985, to three hundred thousand people.

In each of our countless lives since beginningless time, we must have had parents. At one time or another, every single sentient being must have been our mother or father. When we think of all these beings who have been our parents wandering helplessly and for so long in the circle of existence, like blind people who have lost their way, we cannot but feel tremendous compassion for them. Compassion by itself, however, is not enough; they need actual help. But as long as our minds are still limited by attachment, just giving them food, clothing, money, or simply affection will only bring them a limited and temporary happiness at best. What we must do is to find a way to liberate them completely from suffering. This can be done only by following a spiritual path and transforming ourselves so that we can transform others.

Compassion should be directed impartially toward all sentient beings without discriminating between those who are friends and those who are enemies. With this compassion constantly in mind, every positive act, even the offering of a single flower or the recitation of a single mantra, we should do with the wish that it may benefit all living creatures without exception.

The great teachers of the past considered the most precious teaching to be the inseparability of voidness and compassion. They cultivated love, compassion, joy, and equanimity—the four limitless thoughts out of which the ability to help others arises effortlessly. Motivated by compassion for all beings, we should establish firmly in our hearts the intention to attain enlightenment for the sake of others. Without this intention, our compassion will be a pale imitation of the real thing. It is said, "To wish happiness for others, even for those who want to do us harm, is the source of consummate happiness." When finally we reach this level, compassion for all beings arises by itself in a way that is utterly uncontrived.

It is very important to focus our whole being on our commitment to achieve Buddhahood for the sake of others, until it becomes clear just how meaningless and frustrating the activities of this life really are. We will be touched and saddened by the debilitated condition of beings in these difficult times, and a strong feeling of determination to be free from samsara will arise. If these attitudes truly take root, the qualities and achievements of the Great Vehicle are sure to grow from them. But if that genuine determination to be free from samsara is not firmly implanted in our mind, our Dharma practice will never be able to develop fully.

All sentient beings are the same in wishing to be happy and not to suffer. The great difference between myself and others is in numbers—there is only one of me, but countless others. So, my happiness and my suffering are completely insignificant compared to the happiness and suffering of infinite other beings. What truly matters is whether other beings are happy or suffering. This is the basis of the mind determined to attain enlightenment. We should wish others to be happy rather than ourselves, and we should especially wish happiness for those whom we perceive as enemies and those who treat us badly. Otherwise, what is the use of compassion?

Khyentse Rinpoche

Monks pray under the welcome shade of the huge Bodhi tree in Bodhgaya, in the modern Indian state of Bihar, during the annual Nyingma prayer festival.

Under a tree on this site, Buddha Shakyamuni attained enlightenment at the age of thirty-five (see page 36). This is therefore a place of pilgrimage for Buddhists world-

wide. Behind the tree rises the steep Mahabodhi stupa. It is said that all the Buddhas of the past and future attained or will attain enlightenment at the same spot.

KHYENTSE RINPOCHE, THE BUILDER

Each of Khyentse Rinpoche's achievements in different fields seems more than enough to have filled a whole lifetime. Twenty years or so spent practicing in retreat; an astonishing depth and breadth of teaching, taking up at least several hours a day over half a century; twenty-five large volumes of written works; numerous major projects to preserve and disseminate Buddhist thought, tradition, and culture overseen by him—in all these undertakings, Khyentse Rinpoche tirelessly gave form to his lifelong dedication to Buddhism.

His knowledge of the enormous range of Tibetan Buddhist literature was probably unparalleled, and he inherited Jamyang Khyentse Wangpo's determination to preserve and make available texts of all traditions, particularly those in danger of disappearing. Whereas in Jamyang Khyentse Wangpo's time the teachings had been endangered principally by sectarian strife and neglect from within, Khyentse Rinpoche's lifetime saw Tibet's unique heritage threatened from the outside—by the great upheavals of the Chinese invasion and the Cultural Revolution. Innumerable books in countless monastery libraries were systematically destroyed, and few of the lamas and scholars who fled into exile managed to bring their precious books with them on the hurried and hazardous journey, often arriving with little more than the clothes they stood up in. In most cases, nevertheless, the texts survived, even if in only one or very few copies. Even today, lost texts are still turning up. In the late sixties, gradually gathering momentum over two decades as the funds and manpower became available, the huge task of republishing almost the whole of Tibetan literature began. Khyentse Rinpoche himself, through his efforts over the years to edit and publish important texts, preserved nearly three hundred volumes for posterity.

Often complementing or shedding light on the works of great masters of the past, Khyentse Rinpoche's own writings form a veritable encyclopedia of practice texts, commentaries, prayers, poems, and advice. Wherever he was, the book he was currently writing, editing, or correcting was always close at hand. Indeed, he often wrote while receiving people or directing other undertakings, each separate task apparently receiving his undivided attention.

But Khyentse Rinpoche was more than just a great scholar. There is no doubt that what he considered most important, and what gave him the greatest satisfaction, was that the teachings he had himself not only preserved and published, but also practiced, realized, and transmitted, were put into practice by others. It is no surprise, therefore, that he devoted considerable efforts to founding and sustaining temples, colleges, and monasteries where study and practice of the Buddhist tradition could be undertaken. One of his last great tasks was the founding of a new Shechen Monastery in Nepal. He had no interest in setting up a grandiose seat for himself, and to him it truly made no difference whether he lived in a cramped hut or in a vast palace—indeed, during his life he had known both. It was, rather, with an eye to the future that he undertook this major project.

In 1980 Khyentse Rinpoche's wife and Trulshik Rinpoche, his main disciple, suggested to him that he build a small monastery in Nepal as the future seat of his grandson and spiritual heir, Shechen Rabjam Rinpoche. After pondering this idea for a while, Khyentse Rinpoche replied with a big smile that he would build not a small monastery, but one as large as possible. He chose to build this second Shechen Monastery near the Great Stupa of Jarung Kashor in Bodhnath, fulfilling a prediction that a Nyingma monastery built on this site would be a source of great benefit for the Buddhist teaching, and in particular would foster peace and prosperity throughout the region.

Land was soon acquired and the building work began. The twelve years that it took to complete the monastery were a rich combination of artistic creativity, applied traditional knowledge, and joyful effort. As soon as the main building

The new Shechen Monastery in Nepal under construction—and already in use for extensive ceremonies.

started to go up, as many as fifty sculptors, painters, goldsmiths, silversmiths, tailors, mask makers, and builders—all disciples of Khyentse Rinpoche—flocked to the site from all over Bhutan, Tibet, and India to take part in the work.

Khyentse Rinpoche insisted that all aspects of the task be carried out with the greatest care and attention to detail. One hundred and fifty statues were made at the monastery, ranging in height from two to twenty feet. They are hollowed-out structures of clay mixed with handmade paper for strength. Inside is placed the "life-tree," the trunk of a tree, planed to a square cross-section and oriented inside the statue just as it had been when growing in the wild, respecting top and bottom and with the side that had been facing east toward the front of the statue. The life-tree is sanded and polished smooth, painted with vermilion, and inscribed in specific places with mantras in fine gold paint. Relics of past saints— hair, bone fragments, clothing—are attached to the tree, which is then wrapped in fine yellow silk before being set in place. All the space around it is packed with tightly rolled strips of saffron-painted paper on which mantras and prayers have been printed in tiny characters. Pebbles, dried flowers, and medicinal plants from sacred places, pieces of gold, silver, coral, turquoise, and many other precious substances are also placed inside. Finally, when the statue is completely full, the bottom is sealed and a consecration ceremony is performed.

Other sacred objects are made of gilt copper, such as the Wheel of Dharma flanked by a deer and a doe (to commemorate the Buddha Shakyamuni's first teaching, or "turning of the Wheel of Dharma," in the deer park at Varanasi). Gilding is carried out with great skill by traditional methods. First, gold is laminated into fine sheets. Then, over several painstaking days, it is ground in a mor-

tar with mercury to form an amalgam. This amalgam is applied to the copper and the surface heated strongly with a blowtorch. The mercury evaporates and the gold is precipitated. For clay statues, the gilt surface is then polished with an agate stone. Mercury fumes are very toxic, and Tibetan goldsmiths believe that drinking quantities of millet beer after the gilding process helps them eliminate the poison from their system more easily!

The walls of the three main temples of the Shechen Monastery are covered with beautiful frescoes that depict the history of Buddhism in Tibet and portray all the important teachers of the four main schools of Tibetan Buddhism. Under Khyentse Rinpoche's constant direction, the work was executed by two master painters with the help of a dozen assistants.

Altogether, Khyentse Rinpoche performed a hundred ceremonies to consecrate the images and paintings. Such ceremonies involve calling the wisdom, compassion, and power of the particular aspect of the Buddha depicted to dissolve inseparably into its material representation, just as a mind gives life to an inert body.

Wherever he was, Khyentse Rinpoche would rise well before dawn to pray and meditate for several hours before embarking on an uninterrupted flow of activities until late into the night. He accomplished a tremendous daily workload with total serenity and apparent effortlessness.

A typical day began at half past four in the morning. As Khyentse Rinpoche awoke, an attendant, who would have been sleeping on a mat in his room, folded Rinpoche's bedding and served him a cup of hot water and some consecrated pills. Khyentse Rinpoche would then unwrap his prayer book, which contained

A statue, laid on its back, at the final stage of being filled with mantras and relics (see text).

The sand mandala is dissolved at the end of a nine-day ritual (see caption opposite).

over five hundred loose pages, interspersed with fragments written in the handwriting of great masters of the past, miniature paintings, photographs of other great teachers, and dried flowers from sacred pilgrimage places. Until nine o'clock, Khyentse Rinpoche would practice various meditations, visualizations, and prayers. For long periods he would recite the mantra that goes with each practice, counting his recitations with the beads of one of several different rosaries of *bodhi* seeds, crystal, coral, and so forth, according to the nature and purpose of that particular recitation. All these prayers and mantras he recited mentally, without speaking a word. At around half past seven, his attendant would bring him a bowl of roasted barley and salted butter tea.

At nine, Rinpoche would break his morning silence and move to a larger room to receive people, some of whom would already have been gathering outside. Depending on their needs, he would give them spiritual guidance, practical advice, teachings, or blessings; consecrate statues or paintings commissioned for their household shrines; and meet and exchange news with visitors from afar, travelers from Tibet, Bhutanese pilgrims, or messengers sent by other lamas.

When a major ceremony was being performed, Rinpoche would go to the main temple early in the morning to join the two hundred monks assembled there. For the rest of the day he would remain cross-legged on his throne. During the breaks, without moving from his seat, he would conclude his morning prayers, receive visitors, and continue writing the text he was currently working on.

But Khyentse Rinpoche's chief activity was clearly teaching. He taught in every free moment of the day, tirelessly responding to all requests for instruction and spiritual guidance. He would often teach all day for months on end to gatherings ranging from a few dozen to several thousand people. Even after a full day of teaching, he would grant some individual request and teach one person or a small group in his room until late at night. During all-day rituals, while everyone else took their lunch break, he would eat quickly and use every remaining minute before the ceremony resumed to give someone an explanation of a few pages of a meditation text or philosophical commentary. He never turned down any such request. If it was impossible to fit into his schedule, he would send for the person whenever a lull next occurred in his program, or give him an appointment the next day. Because of the abundance of such requests and Rinpoche's willingness to satisfy them all, it would often happen that half a dozen people would turn up at the same time the next day!

Anyone who ever heard Khyentse Rinpoche teach was struck by his remarkable delivery. Glancing rarely at the written text, he would speak effortlessly at a steady rate, evenly, without strong emphasis, in a ceaseless stream with no pause or hesitation, as if reading from an unseen book in his memory. Somehow the subject would always be uniformly covered from beginning to end, in just the allocated time, pitched precisely at the audience's level of understanding. Spoken by him, even a few simple words could open the door to a whole succession of new insights into spiritual life. His immense knowledge, the warmth of his blessings, and the depth of his inner realization gave his teachings a quality quite different from those of any other teacher.

Profoundly gentle and patient though he was, Khyentse Rinpoche's presence, his vastness of mind, and powerful physical appearance, inspired awe and respect. With close disciples and attendants he could be very strict, for he knew that a good disciple "grows strong under strong discipline." He never spoke harshly to visitors or those not committed to him, but with his own disciples he was uncompromising in making sure that they never got away with shabby behavior, words, and thoughts. To those living near him, it was also somehow obvious that he could see clearly through any pretense or hypocrisy. Although the Buddhist teachings point out that there is no better witness than one's own mind, his loving yet formidable presence had a powerful influence on his disciples and ensured that their minds did not wander.

Many great men and women, apart from their particular genius in science or the arts, are not necessarily good human beings. Khyentse Rinpoche was someone whose greatness was totally in accord with the teachings he professed. However unfathomable the depth and breadth of his mind might seem, from an ordinary point of view he was an extraordinarily good human being. Those who lived near him, even for ten or fifteen years, say that they never witnessed a single word or deed of his that harmed anyone. His only concern was the present and ultimate benefit of others. Here was a living example of what lay at the end of the spiritual path—the greatest possible inspiration for anyone thinking of setting out on the journey to enlightenment.

Shechen Monastery in Bodhnath, Nepal. At the end of a long drupchen *ceremony lasting nine consecutive days and nights, the mandala, drawn in precise detail with different colored sand, is swept up* (**opposite**) *as a symbol of the impermanence of all phenomena. The sand is placed in an urn and carried in procession to be scattered in a nearby river. The procession returns to the monastery courtyard, and the monks walk in single file in the form known as the "circle of joy"* (gakhyil)—*resembling the Chinese yin-yang symbol—before going back into the temple for the conclusion.*

Monks with ceremonial drums walk in procession around the Great Stupa of Jarungkashor, Bodhnath, in Nepal's Kathmandu valley. The stupa is a major pilgrimage place for Tibetan Buddhists, for its construction was linked to the establishment of Buddhism in Tibet. According to ancient legend, the four sons of the poultry-woman Shamvara who built the stupa were reborn as the Guru Padmasambhava, the Abbot Shantarakshita, the King Trisong Detsen (see page 38), and the minister Bami Trihzi, as the result of wishes they made on completing the stupa.

As an offering, devotees regularly sponsor the whitewashing of the stupa, concluded by the scattering of saffron-colored water in wide arcs around the "vase" of the monument and the hanging of new prayer flags from its pinnacle.

Khyentse Rinpoche sits on the steps of the Great Stupa of Bodhnath, surrounded by some of the many incarnate lamas who gathered in Nepal in 1977 to receive an extensive cycle of empowerments and teachings from him. The different ceremonial hats worn by some of the lamas are characteristic of the tradition to which they belong. Khyentse Rinpoche himself is wearing the "Lotus Crown" resembling the hat worn by Guru Padmasambhava.

The gold of the stupa's pinnacle, gleaming brightly in the morning sun, was offered by a wandering Tibetan yogi, Shabkar, in 1821.

Khyentse Rinpoche watches the annual sacred dance festival from his window on the first floor of Shechen Monastery in Nepal.

The sacred dance festival at Shechen Monastery in Nepal, celebrating the anniversary of Guru Padmasambhava, is the same as that held at Shechen Monastery in Tibet (pictured on pages 22–27). The dance masters from Tibet came to Nepal to teach the complex dances, lasting for two full days.

A dancer in his five-petaled crown, symbolizing the five wisdom Buddhas, his face half-hidden behind black strands that represent the hair of the dakini *(sky-going female enlightened beings) whose role he is playing.*

The Buddhist teachings describe three fundamental attitudes, corresponding to the three paths, or *yanas* ("vehicles"), which can be practiced together as an integrated whole.

Renunciation, the foundation of the Basic Vehicle and therefore at the root of all subsequent stages of the path, implies the strong wish to free oneself not only from life's immediate sorrows but from the seemingly unending sufferings of samsara, the vicious cycle of conditioned existence. With it comes a heartfelt weariness and disillusionment with the endless quest for gratification, approval, profit, and status.

Compassion, the driving force of the Great Vehicle, is born as one realizes that both the individual "self" and the appearances of the phenomenal world are actually devoid of any intrinsic, independent existence; one sees all the suffering that results from one's own and others' fundamental ignorance, which misconstrues the infinite display of illusory appearances as being composed of separate, permanently existing entities. An enlightened being—one who has understood this absence of any intrinsic, independent existence as the ultimate nature of all things—naturally acts from the boundless compassion he feels for those who, under the spell of ignorance, are wandering and suffering in samsara. Inspired by a similar compassion, the follower of the Great Vehicle does not aim for his own liberation alone, but vows to attain Buddhahood in order to attain the capacity to free all sentient beings from the suffering inherent in samsara.

Pure perception, the extraordinary outlook of the Adamantine Vehicle, is to recognize the Buddha-nature in all sentient beings and to see primordial purity and perfection in all phenomena. Every sentient being is endowed with the essence of Buddhahood, just as oil pervades every sesame seed. Ignorance is simply to be unaware of this Buddha-nature, like a poor man who does not know that there is a pot of gold buried beneath his hovel. The journey to enlightenment is thus a rediscovery of this forgotten nature, like seeing the ever-brilliant sun again as the clouds that have been hiding it are blown away.

Khyentse Rinpoche

Khyentse Rinpoche visits Thang-boche Monastery, near Everest base camp in Nepal, and from the monastery window watches sacred dances being held in his honor in the courtyard below, along with his host Thangboche Rinpoche (left). *All around are spectacular views of the mountains* (see pages 95–97).

Twenty-one lamas in the "black hat" costume wait to go outside into the monastery courtyard to perform one of the sacred dances.

A mask representing one of the eight manifestations of Guru Padmasambhava called Nyimai Özer, "Light Rays of the Sun." More than one hundred different masks, made by one of monastery's resident artists, are used in the sacred dances.

A chant master from Shechen Monastery in Tibet who came to teach ritual chants to the young monks of Shechen Monastery in Nepal. He accompanies this particular chant with domed rolmo *cymbals.*

The source of all phenomena of samsara and nirvana
Is the nature of mind—void, luminous,
All-encompassing, vast as the sky.

When in that state of skylike vastness,
Relax into its openness; stay in that very openness,
Merge with that skylike state:
Naturally, it will become more and more relaxed—
Wonderful!

If you become accomplished
In this method of integrating mind with view,
Your realization will naturally become vast.
And just as the sun shines freely throughout space,
Your compassion cannot fail to shine on all unrealized beings.

Khyentse Rinpoche

The qualities of buddhahood pervade all beings just as oil pervades a sesame seed. These qualities have always been there, complete and never-changing, as the naturally radiant expression of the absolute nature. In that sense, it can be said that all the qualities of nirvana are completely present throughout samsara, the realm of suffering and delusion, as well. What is the relationship between the phenomena of delusion and those of enlightenment? Consider clouds in the sky. When clouds form, they do so thanks to the sky. Yet the sky never changes; clouds manifest within it, and then, when they are dispersed by the wind, the sky reappears just as it has always been. In the same way, no phenomena, even those of samsara, are ever relinquished by the enlightened nature of nirvana. They manifest within that enlightened nature but do not modify it in any way.

Are the phenomena of enlightenment, therefore, also permeated by the phenomena of delusion? No, they are not, because the absolute nature never changes. It cannot be affected by any amount of delusion. So, we can say that the phenomena of delusion are never other than the absolute nature, yet the absolute nature does not contain the phenomena of delusion. The buddha-nature is present in delusion, but delusion is not present in the buddha-nature.

As the *Guhyagarbha Tantra* says, "The absolute nature is veiled by the formation of thoughts." Beings have forgotten the absolute, their own true nature. The absolute nature is like the sun, and phenomena are like the rays of light that emanate from it. To recognize that all these rays of light, phenomena, come from the sun, the absolute nature itself, is to be totally enlightened at that very moment. But unenlightened beings, not recognizing where the rays are coming from, turn their backs to the sun, and instead of looking at the light rays' source they look at where they fall. They start to create the notion of an object out there and a subject within. Then, when the five senses connect the 'object' to the 'subject,' craving and aversion arise; the seeds of samsara have been sown, and from them grow the three realms of samsaric existence. But at no point have the phenomena of delusion been separated from the nature of buddhahood, which always pervades each and every being, and all phenomena.

Just as the whole world, with its mountains, continents, and everything else, exists within infinite space, so too do all phenomena appear within the buddha-nature. Space, within which the whole universe appears, does not need to show itself in any way to whatever is taking place within it. In the same way, the buddhas in their enlightened nature do not need to manifest in any way. Yet, through the links created by the powerful aspirations they conceived just before achieving enlightenment and by beings' prayers to them for their blessings, the buddhas spontaneously appear in various ways to help beings according to their needs.

The phenomena of enlightenment and those of delusion are both included within the absolute nature, therefore—but that absolute nature is never stained or obscured by the delusion of relative phenomena.

Khyentse Rinpoche

An artist applies paint of real gold to an enormous statue of the Buddha in the main temple of Shechen Monastery in Nepal. The interior of the statue has already been filled with relics and mantras, and when all the gold has been applied the statue will be polished with an agate stone to bring out its full luster. The temple contains three such huge statues, representing the Buddha of the present, Shakyamuni, flanked by one of the Buddhas of the past, Dipamkara, and the coming future Buddha, Maitreya.

At the end of a long ceremony, the lamas perform an offering of butter lamps. Each person holds a lighted lamp and is linked to his neighbors with white scarves which, knotted together, run through the whole assembly. The participants recite slow and melodious verses in which they pray to practice together throughout their future lives until they all attain enlightenment.

At the beginning of a drupchen *ceremony in the temple of Shechen Monastery in Nepal, Rabjam Rinpoche consecrates the place on the altar where the sand mandala will be created. He consecrates it by standing there, visualizing himself as the mandala's central deity while reciting the ritual text.*

Phenomena are the radiance of the innate absolute;
Mind's nature is the wisdom of the innate absolute.
The ultimate teacher—phenomena and mind merged in one taste—
Dwells naturally within myself. Ah ho! What a joy!

Khyentse Rinpoche

(above) *Khyentse Rinpoche with his close friend and disciple Trulshik Rinpoche, who was later to discover his incarnation* (see pages 142 and 148). *When two great masters meet like this, they not only discuss deep philosophical points but also tease each other, exchange news, and tell stories, all in an atmosphere of overflowing joy, natural warmth, and good humor.*

(opposite) *Khyentse Rinpoche, assisted by Rabjam Rinpoche, gives the basic Buddhist vows of refuge to a group of young monks who have recently joined the monastery. At the end of the ceremony, he cuts the remaining lock of hair from their shaved heads and gives them new names.*

All appearances are vast openness,
Blissful and utterly free.

With a free, happy mind
I sing this song of joy.

When one looks toward one's own mind—
The root of all phenomena—
There is nothing but vivid emptiness,
Nothing concrete there to be taken as real.

It is present as transparent, utter openness,
Without outside, without inside—
An all-pervasiveness
Without boundary and without direction.

The wide-open expanse of the view,
The true condition of mind,
Is like the sky, like space:
Without center, without edge, without goal.

By leaving whatever I experience
Relaxed in ease, just as it is,
I have arrived at the vast plain
That is the absolute expanse.

Dissolving into the expanse of emptiness
That has no limits and no boundary,
Everything I see, everything I hear,
My own mind, and the sky all merge.

Not once has the notion arisen
Of these being separate and distinct.

In the absolute expanse of awareness
All things are blended into that single taste—
But, relatively, each and every phenomenon is distinctly,
    clearly seen.
Wondrous!

Shabkar

Without a center, without an edge,
The luminous expanse of awareness that encompasses all—
This vivid, bright vastness:
Natural, primordial presence.

Without an inside, without an outside,
Awareness arisen of itself, as wide as the sky,
Beyond size, beyond direction, beyond limits—
This utter, complete openness:
Space, inseparable from awareness.

Within that birthless, wide-open expanse of space,
Phenomena appear—like rainbows, utterly transparent.
Pure and impure realms, Buddhas and sentient beings
Are seen, brilliant and distinct.

As far as the sky pervades, so does awareness.
As far as awareness extends, so does absolute space.

Sky, awareness, absolute space,
Indistinguishably intermixed:
Immense, infinitely vast—
The ground of samsara,
The ground of nirvana.
To remain, day and night, in this state—
To enter this state easily—this is joy.
Emaho!

Shabkar

*Khyentse Rinpoche wearing the robes of Guru Padmasambhava
and making his symbolic gestures.*

92

The Great Stupa of Bodhnath in Nepal (see page 78), *from a monastery roof on which, in the foreground, can be seen the Wheel of Dharma flanked by two attentive deer, a symbol of the occasion when the Buddha first taught in the deer park at Sarnath, near Varanasi in India.*

In the vicinity of the Great Stupa are sixteen Tibetan Buddhist monasteries, many with colleges offering advanced study courses of nine or twelve years, making this one of the most thriving centers of Buddhist learning in the world.

Snow lions don't freeze in snow mountains;
Vultures don't fall out of the sky;
Fish don't drown in water;
Practitioners don't die of hunger.
So cast away this life's concerns!
Give up plans for the future!

Shabkar

If I do not give away
My happiness for others' pain,
Enlightenment will never be attained,
And even in samsara, joy will fly from me.

Shantideva

The Stupa of Swayambunath, on top of a small hill to the west of Kathmandu. One of the three great stupas in the Kathmandu valley, it is said to have been built in the time of the previous Buddha, Kashyapa, and is highly venerated by Buddhists throughout the Himalayan region.

*Carried on a litter by the Sherpa
monks of Thangboche Monastery
in the Everest region in Nepal,
Khyentse Rinpoche passes through
the monastery entrance. In the*
*background, beyond the sharp
peak of Ama Dablam, lies the
mountain range marking the
border with Tibet.*

This secluded mountain place:
Above—a slow, soft rain drizzles down.
Flocks of eagles flying—north, south—
Rainbows vividly appear.

Below me—the curved necks of geese
Glancing, and the river flowing on, sinuous.
Behind them, deer dance on the slope
Of a mountain whose peak penetrates space.

On both sides, meadows blaze with wildflowers;
Myriad bees whirl above them.
In front, rocks ornament the mountain meadows;
A cuckoo's call fills me with sadness.

Today I climbed behind
This excellent retreat place,
I raised my head, looking up,
And saw the cloudless sky.

I thought of absolute space, free from limits,
I then experienced a freedom
Without center, without end—
All biased views
Completely abandoned.

I lowered my head to look in front of me,
And saw the sun of this world.
I thought of meditation—
Luminous and unobscured.
I then experienced a non-dual, empty clarity.
All meditations that focus the mind
Completely abandoned.

I turned my head, looking south,
And saw a pattern of rainbows.
I thought of all phenomena—
At once both apparent and empty.
I then experienced a non-dual, natural clarity.
All nihilist and eternalist viewpoints
Completely abandoned.

Shabkar

(opposite) *The peak of Ama Dablam and its plunging glacier, seen from Thangboche Monastery.*

(above) *Lama Ngödrup, Khyentse Rinpoche's close attendant and bursar for twenty-five years, surveys the Khumbu valley from a rock above Thangboche Monastery. Behind him, prayer flags, hung from a clump of growing bamboo stems, sway in the wind.*

RETURN TO TIBET

It was in 1985 that Khyentse Rinpoche at last returned to Shechen. Waiting for him several hours from his destination, in the brilliant light of Eastern Tibet at twelve thousand feet above sea level, were three hundred horsemen with tanned faces, wearing white hats and holding multicolored banners flapping in the wind. These were not warriors, but monks who had come to welcome him home after thirty years in exile. When Rinpoche's car arrived, they walked their horses slowly around it in a vast circle, taking off their hats as they passed in front of him, and then left at a gallop for the monastery to be ready to receive him there. Not only monks had come; all the nomads in the region left their black yak-hair tents and hurried down from the hillsides to stand by the road. Lighting branches of juniper and fir to make fragrant white incense smoke, each small group hoped to stop Khyentse Rinpoche's car and receive his blessing. Here, where the temperature is often minus forty, the nomads wear thick sheepskins to withstand the rigors of winter. The women wear ornaments of coral, turquoise, and amber in their hair, and carry in the folds of their coats children with cheeks reddened by the winter winds. From their belts hang flint lighters, with tinder made from petals of the edelweiss that grows in the mountain pastures.

Only ruins remained of the monastery. As Rinpoche approached, the music of strident oboes, clanging cymbals, and the deep roar of fifteen-foot-long trumpets burst into life from the roof of the monastic college—the only building standing amidst the ruins—filling the valley with majestic echoes. A long procession of monks and musicians led Khyentse Rinpoche to the temple. As soon as he had taken his seat, a crowd of monks and laypeople filed past, gazing at him with a fervor that welled up from their very bones. As they received his blessing and looked up at him, few of them, especially the older people, could any longer hold back their tears. Some muttered a few words, or told him their name. Khyentse Rinpoche smiled at them, every now and then recognizing a face from the past. After

several hours, when what seemed to be an unending flow had finally died down, he conversed with the monastery's elders around a pot of boiling butter tea. They had so much to tell him—about their unspeakable ordeal in the hands of the Chinese Communists, about who had died and who had survived—but on that day the first priority was the joy of meeting again. For them, it was like a sudden bright sunrise after a long night of darkness.

Starting the very next day, a two-day festival of sacred dances began in honor of Khyentse Rinpoche's return. More than a hundred dancers and musicians, all monks of the monastery, took part. The dance festival used to be a traditional high point in the monastery's year, but for many years under Chinese occupation it had been unthinkable. Only the year before, for the first time, had the older monks dared to revive the tradition, and the dancers' shining brocade costumes and beautiful masks, all of which had been destroyed, had been made anew.

At the end of the dances, Khyentse Rinpoche gave blessings and teachings to the monks and laypeople who had come to meet him from all over Eastern Tibet. Amidst his attentive audience stood out faces of astonishing character and beauty, rock solid, their gaze as clear as the sky. Old monks tirelessly turned enormous prayer wheels. All around the valley, the visitors' horses and the yaks dotted the slopes with brown, black, and white.

Khyentse Rinpoche insisted on spending a night at the spot high above the monastery where the hermitage of his main teacher, Shechen Gyaltsap, had formerly stood. He could no longer walk unaided and had to be carried up the hill. There was hardly any trace left of the hermitage, but he camped on the small platform under the stars and everyone else slept here and there in the forest and in nearby caves. On the precipitous slope, some feared they might roll downhill during their sleep. Later a small hermitage was rebuilt on the site.

Other monasteries invited Khyentse Rinpoche to visit, and he agreed to travel wherever he could. Where there was no road, he was carried on a litter or in a sedan chair. For several days the party crossed passes of over fifteen thousand feet, traversed precipices, and waded across rivers. Everyone wanted the honor of carrying the lama, and with a new and enthusiastic team taking over every quarter of an hour the long distances were covered fast. At each monastery, the same elaborate and dignified reception awaited. The monks, in their white hats as a sign of welcome, together with the whole local populace, formed a long procession in single file, preceded by musicians in their multicolored ceremonial costumes. As the procession arrived at the foot of Dzongsar Monastery, everyone suddenly looked up at the sky. A luminescent halo had formed around the sun, a sign Tibetans consider as very auspicious. The day before it had been a double rainbow, rising up from the roofs of Palpung Monastery, that had greeted Khyentse Rinpoche as he arrived there (see page 122).

Everywhere he went, Rinpoche taught, comforted, and inspired all who came to see him. The teaching of Buddhism is not based on some exotic, inaccessible philosophy. It deals with the most basic mechanisms of happiness and suffering, and shows how true and lasting happiness can come only from inner peace. Such peace can be reached only by cultivating unselfishness, love, and compassion, and by eliminating egotism, hatred, and greed.

Khyentse Rinpoche was greeted everywhere he went during this first visit and two subsequent visits to Eastern and Central Tibet with an astonishing degree of fervor. For the Tibetans these visits had enormous significance, and they could hardly believe their own eyes. Many of them cried out, "We must be dreaming!" For over thirty years they had been holding firm in the teeth of so much suffering. Their faith and determination had not given way even an inch.

While in Central Tibet in 1985, Khyentse Rinpoche submitted a petition to the Chinese government asking permission for Samye Monastery to be restored, stressing its importance for the world's cultural heritage. Samye was Tibet's first Buddhist monastery, founded in the eighth century by Guru Padmasambhava and the Abbot Shantarakshita under the patronage of King Trisong Detsen. Surprisingly enough, the Chinese government agreed. Inspired by Khyentse Rinpoche, the king of Bhutan contributed a large donation to the undertaking. So it was that by 1990, Samye's main temple building had been restored right up to its dazzling golden roofs. Khyentse Rinpoche was invited to reconsecrate the monastery, and traveled again to Tibet. At Samye he performed an elaborate three-day consecration ceremony, at the same time giving teachings and initiations to the monastery's sixty monks and to all those who had gathered for this unique occasion, including a group of Western disciples. Much restoration work still remained to be done—the eight satellite temples in the eight directions around the central building, four huge stupas, and a hundred and eight smaller stupas that had formerly crowned the perimeter wall. In Lhasa, Rinpoche made offerings of two hundred thousand butter lamps in the temple of the famous Crowned Buddha, the Jowo Rinpoche, before touring a number of sacred places and monastic centers in Central Tibet. This was to be his last journey to Tibet.

Although Khyentse Rinpoche had by now turned eighty, his characteristic stamina seemed little affected. However, in early 1991 he began to show the first signs of ill health while teaching in Bodh Gaya. Completing his program there nevertheless, he traveled to Dharamsala and without apparent difficulty spent a month giving important empowerments and transmissions to the Dalai Lama, which the latter had been requesting for many years.

Back in Nepal, as spring advanced, it became obvious that his health was steadily deteriorating. He was losing weight and needed more and more rest. He passed much of the time in silent prayer and meditation, setting aside only a few hours of the day to meet those who most needed to see him. He was obliged to cancel a fourth journey to Tibet, where he had planned to visit Shechen Monastery once again. Instead, he chose to spend three and a half months in retreat opposite the Tiger's Nest, Paro Taktsang, in Bhutan, one of the most sacred places blessed by Padmasambhava.

After his retreat, Rinpoche seemed to be in better health. He visited several of his disciples who were in retreat and spoke to them of the ultimate teacher, beyond birth and death or any physical manifestation. But shortly afterward he was again showing signs of illness, and for twelve days was almost completely unable to eat or drink. On September 27,1991, at nightfall, he asked his attendants to help him sit in an upright position and went into a peaceful sleep. In the early hours of the morning, his breathing ceased and his mind dissolved in the absolute expanse.

Thus Khyentse Rinpoche's extraordinary life came to an end, a life spent entirely in study, practice, and teaching from an early age. Wherever he was, day or night, in the same uninterrupted flow of kindness, humor, wisdom, and dignity, his every effort had been directed to the preservation and expression of all forms of the Buddhist teaching.

At the request of disciples from Tibet and all over the world, his body was preserved for a year, using traditional embalming methods. It was also taken from Bhutan to Shechen Monastery in Nepal for several months, so that more people could come to pay their respects. Every Friday (the day of his death) for the first seven weeks, one hundred thousand butter lamps were offered on the Bodhnath stupa near Shechen Monastery. The whole Tibetan community joined the monks to help prepare and light the lamps.

Finally, his remains were cremated near Paro in Bhutan, in November 1992, at a three-day ceremony attended by over a hundred important lamas, the royal family and ministers of Bhutan, five hundred Western disciples, and a huge crowd of some fifty thousand devotees—a gathering unprecedented in Bhutan's history.

Khampa monks on horseback,
carrying brightly colored banners
of welcome, wait to escort
Khyentse Rinpoche for the last

ten miles of the road to Shechen
Monastery in Tibet as he returns
after thirty years of exile (see
page 98).

If you conquer the primordial nature by distinguishing mind
   from awareness,
The view of the absolute will gradually become clear.
Even if inwardly awareness is not yet clear right now,
Simply keep the mind from wandering outside;
This will do, for awareness lies in the very depth of the mind.
They are, it is said, like water and ice:
Water and ice are not entirely the same,
For the latter is solid and can be held.
But molten ice is none other than water,
So, in truth, water and ice are not two things, but one.
Likewise mind is not awareness, being deluded,
But mind's nature, when realized, is none other than awareness.
Although mind and awareness are different in sense,
They cannot be distinguished by analytic reasoning.
One day, as your confidence in awareness grows,
Mind will appear as witless as a child
And awareness as wise as a venerable old sage.
Awareness will not run after mind, but eclipse it;
In a relaxed, serene state, rest at ease.

                                    Khyentse Rinpoche

Young novice monks hold flowers to welcome Khyentse Rinpoche.

The monks of Shechen, their cheeks reddened by the icy winds of Eastern Tibet, form a mounted convoy to greet Khyentse Rinpoche as he arrives. Their white hats, made of cotton on a bamboo frame, are worn as a traditional sign of welcome.

Another welcoming procession greets Khyentse Rinpoche's arrival, this time at the sister monastery of Dzogchen. The costumes and masks represent the peoples of different parts of the world, as if everyone on earth had come to welcome the guest.

M ind has no form, no color, and no substance; this is its empty aspect. Yet mind can know things and perceive an infinite variety of phenomena. This is its clear aspect. The inseparability of these two aspects, emptiness and clarity, is the primordial, continuous nature of mind.

At present, the natural clarity of your mind is obscured by delusions. But as the obscuration clears you will begin to uncover the radiance of awareness, until you reach a point where, just as a line traced on water disappears the moment it is made, your thoughts are liberated the moment they arise. To experience mind in this way is to encounter the very source of Buddhahood. When the nature of mind is recognized, that is called nirvana; when it is obscured by delusion, that is called samsara. Yet neither samsara nor nirvana have ever parted from the continuum of the absolute. When awareness reaches its full extent, the ramparts of delusion will have been breached and the citadel of the absolute, beyond meditation, can be seized once and for all.

Khyentse Rinpoche

A twelve-year-old monk, nephew of the chief dance-master, rehearses for the annual festival.

104

A procession of monks at the monastery of Dzachuka, one day's journey from Shechen, play highly reverberant rolmo cymbals. They are made of an alloy of five different metals, and an instrument with a particularly good sound is a treasured monastery possession. The crested hats, known as sersha, are worn by ordinary monks at designated moments during most ceremonies.

At Lagong Monastery in Minyak, Eastern Tibet, near the former border with China, the monks await Khyentse Rinpoche's arrival holding their pure white scarves of greeting. The path is decorated with the eight auspicious symbols drawn in white chalk— the golden fish, the eternal knot, the victory banner, and so on— symbolizing different parts of the Buddha's body. For example, there are the golden fish for his eyes, because just as fish swim through water with open eyes, so too the Buddha crosses samsara with the eyes of wisdom always open.

A stack of wood behind is destined for the continuing rebuilding work, carried out by volunteers from the nomad community.

Khampa faces express the fierce courage, natural goodness and unwavering, visceral devotion typical of this indomitable people, whose character has withstood decades of repression and propaganda under the Chinese occupation.

Realization occurs in three stages: understanding, experiences, and true realization. The first is theoretical understanding and comes from studying the teachings. It is necessary, of course, but it is not very stable. It is like a patch, sewn on a cloth, which will eventually come off. Theoretical understanding is not strong enough to weather the good and bad things that happen to you in life. If difficulties arise, no theoretical understanding will allow you to overcome them.

As for experiences in meditation, they are, like mist, bound to fade away. If you concentrate on your practice in a secluded place, you are sure to have various experiences. But such experiences are very unreliable, and it is said, "Meditators who run after experiences, like a child running after a beautiful rainbow, will be misled." When you practice intensely, you may have flashes of clairvoyance and various signs of accomplishment, but all they do is to foster expectations and pride—they are just devilish tricks and the source of obstacles.

It is said that good circumstances are more difficult to deal with than bad ones, because they are more distracting. If you have whatever you could wish for—wealth, a comfortable house, clothing—you should view it all as illusory, like possessions obtained in a dream, rather than feeling compulsive attachment to it. If someone gets angry with you or threatens you, it is relatively easy to meditate on patience; or, if you fall sick, to cope with the sickness. Since such things are causes of suffering, and suffering naturally reminds us of the Dharma, in a way it's easier to integrate these difficult circumstances into your path. But when things are going well and you feel happy, your mind accepts that situation without any difficulty. Like oil spread all over your skin, attachment easily stays invisibly blended into the mind; it becomes part of your thoughts. Once such attachment to favorable circumstances is present, you become almost infatuated with your achievements, your fame, and your wealth. That is something very difficult to get rid of.

But someone with true realization is like a mighty mountain that cannot be shaken by any wind, or like the unchanging blue sky. Good or adverse circumstances, even in their thousands, will provoke no attachment or aversion, no expectation or doubt at all. It is said in the scriptures that such a person will be no more pleased at having someone on one side of him waving a sandalwood fan than fearful of someone on the other side ready to strike him with an axe. For such a person, all deluded perceptions are exhausted. The result is that all circumstances, whether adverse or favorable, will further his progress on the path.

Khyentse Rinpoche

A large crowd of Shechen monks and visiting laypeople receive a blessing from Khyentse Rinpoche. The monk on the right and his unseen partner play the Tibetan oboe or gyaling *continuously during the two hours that it takes for the consecrated substances to be distributed among the crowd. The* gyaling, *a reed instrument, is played using a special breathing technique called* uk-khor, *"circular breath." It allows continuous, unbroken sounding of the instrument by the expulsion of a reservoir of air held in the inflated cheeks while the lungs are being refilled via the nose.*

The master of a small retreat center attached to Tsatsa Monastery, an hour down the valley from Shechen. Ten retreatants practice the traditional three-year, three-month, three-day program under his guidance in a beautiful retreat center built of white pine logs.

A retreat practitioner, identifiable by his long hair, which has remained uncut since the start of his retreat.

*Two gyaling players precede
Khyentse Rinpoche into the ruins
of Shechen Monastery in 1985.
He is assisted to his feet by one of
his attendant monks and an*
*accompanying Bhutanese
officer, and is closely followed by
his wife Lhamo and grandson
Rabjam Rinpoche.*

Where there is no road, Khyentse Rinpoche is carried on a litter; here his party fords the river *below Shechen Monastery, preceded by a monk bearing the brocade parasol of honor.*

In wild places where no one lives,
Are pleasant caves in which to dwell and practice.

In wild places where no one lives,
One's consoling friends will be wild animals and birds.

In wild places where no one lives,
One's nourishment will be wild roots and berries.

In wild places where no one lives
Is the market where samsara is traded for nirvana.

In wild places where no one lives
Are the conditions favorable for realization.

In wild places where no one lives
Is natural beauty delightful to behold.

There is no possible way to express
The many virtues of staying in remote and lonely places
Far removed from human habitation.

Therefore, heir of the Victorious Ones,
Go to a secluded place and practice!
Shabkar

*Looking down on Shechen Monastery from the hillside above.
This photograph shows the state of the main temple (at far right)
in 1985. Across the river is the monastic college, which had been
a famous center of learning before the Cultural Revolution,
housing a hundred students for a twelve-year curriculum. After a
lapse of thirty years, the college has started up again and now has
forty new students.*

Two khenpos *or scholars, both eminent teachers of Buddhist philosophy and practice at nearby monasteries, who have come to meet Khyentse Rinpoche at*

Shechen. Khenpo Wanglo, on the left, subsequently came to Nepal to teach at Shechen Monastery there, and died in 1992 after returning to Tibet.

Khyentse Rinpoche gives an empowerment to a large group of lamas under a tent at the Shechen Monastic College in 1985. After each stage in the transmission, which requires the participants to *meditate and visualize according to the master's instructions, they approach to receive a blessing by being touched with the different symbolic elements of the ritual, or by drinking a few drops* *of liquid from a ceremonial vase (pumba), decorated with a peacock feather and here seen in Khyentse Rinpoche's hand. In Vajrayana Buddhism, an empowerment, or* wang, *is an* *indispensable transmission that also authorizes the recipient to undertake a particular contemplative practice.*

(above) *During his 1988 visit to Kham, Khyentse Rinpoche spent three days in a sedan chair, traveling from Derge, the capital of Kham, to Dzongsar Monastery. The party crossed several moun-* *tain passes and steep valleys, camping on the way. Here they approach the top of the Gosé-La Pass, described on page 4.*

(right) *Despite his eighty years and the primitive, jolting ride, Khyentse Rinpoche never seems tired on the journey. He is, rather, overjoyed to see the landscape and sacred places of his youth.*

The party stops at the top of the 17,000-foot pass to rest and enjoy the view, shouting "Kihi hi! Lha gyalo!"—"May the gods be victorious!"—the cries customary on crossing such a pass.

In mountain rock mansions,
In the cool shade of forests,
In small huts of green grass,
Under tents of white cotton,
I, the carefree yogin,
Dwell at will.

Here is a cheerful song
From a mind at peace.

Divine authentic guru,
Your kindness to me
Exceeds that of the Buddha!

Entrusting myself to you,
I understood that all appearances
Are the magical play of the mind;
That the phenomena of samsara and nirvana
Are apparent yet unreal.

I realized that the nature of this mind,
The root of samsara and nirvana,
Is an ineffable luminous void
With nothing to cling to.

I stayed in a solitary place
In the continuum of the natural state—
Like releasing a handful of cotton wool,
I let consciousness relax,
And it resumed its natural shape.

The darkness of ignorance
Having naturally cleared,
There arose the vast sky
Of the absolute expanse.

As to whether this is the absolute nature
Not a question, not a hesitation
Arises in my mind.
Even if all the Buddhas were to appear before me,
I would have no doubts for them to clarify.
                                    Shabkar

The teacher is like a great ship carrying us across the perilous ocean of existence, an unerring navigator guiding us to the dry land of liberation, a rain of nectar extinguishing the inferno of negative emotions and actions, a bright sun and moon dispelling the darkness of ignorance, the firm earth patiently bearing the weight of both good and bad, a wish-granting tree bestowing both present and ultimate happiness, a treasury of vast and deep instructions, a wish-granting gem providing whatever beings need on their path, a father and mother loving all beings equally, a great river of wide and swift compassion, a great mountain of joy rising above worldly concerns and unshaken by the winds of emotions, and a great cloud raining down its benefits impartially everywhere, uninfluenced by like or dislike. To make any connection with him, whether seeing him, hearing his voice, remembering him, or being touched by his hand, will lead us toward liberation. To have full confidence in him is the surest way to progress toward enlightenment. The warmth of his wisdom and compassion will melt the ore of our being to release the gold of the Buddha-nature within.

Khyentse Rinpoche

On the relative level the teacher appears in human form, gives teachings, and shows us the path. Through his instructions and by his blessing a time will come when his realization and ours will become one. At that time we will realize that the absolute inner teacher has always been present as the nature of our mind.

Jamgön Kongtrul

Unless the sun of devotion shines
On the snow peak of the teacher's four *kayas*,
The stream of his blessings will never flow.
So earnestly arouse devotion in your mind!
Drikung Kyobpa

Better than meditating on a hundred thousand deities
For ten million *kalpas*
Is to think of one's teacher for a single instant.
Precious Embodiment Tantra

During his journey between
Derge and Dzongsar, Khyentse
Rinpoche's party came across
a small tent pitched by members
of a local branch of the Dilgo

family, who had prepared a
small reception for him there.
The party stopped there for a
brief rest and refreshment.
Family members of all ages—

many in tears—of whom only
the older people had known
him in the past, met Khyentse
Rinpoche and exchanged news.

*A few hours before Khyentse
Rinpoche's arrival at Dzongsar
Monastery, former seat of his
teacher Khyentse Chökyi Lodrö,
a thousand horsemen wait to
escort Khyentse Rinpoche, with
the young incarnation of Chökyi
Lodrö who has accompanied him
from India, the rest of the way to
the monastery.*

From June to late August in Eastern Tibet the meadows of the
rolling pasturelands are carpeted
with flowers, first yellow butter-
cups, then blue gentians and

marjoram and white edelweiss.
Khyentse Rinpoche stops during
his journey for a rest, and talks to
Zenkar Rinpoche and Pewar
Rinpoche, two lamas who have

contributed much knowledge and
energy to the revival of Buddhism
in Eastern Tibet.

Just as silvery mist rises
Into the vast, empty firmament,
Will not the form of the lord guru
Appear in the immensity of all-pervading space?

Just as gentle rain slowly descends
Within the beautiful arc of a rainbow,
Will not the guru shower down profound teachings
Within a dome of five-colored light?

Just as rainwater remains
Upon the even ground of a broad meadow,
Will not these teachings remain in the mind
Of your faithful and devoted son?

Just as brilliantly colored flowers
Spring up across the lush, soft moorland,
Will not spiritual experiences and realization
Arise in your son's mindstream?

Shabkar

*A double rainbow appears over Palpung Monastery as Khyentse
Rinpoche's party approaches. Tibetans consider rainbows to be
very auspicious signs.*

I have shown you the methods
That lead to liberation.
But you should know
That liberation depends upon yourself.
Buddha Shakyamuni

The mind, dividing experience into subject and object, first identifies with the subject, "I," then with the idea of "mine," and starts to cling to "my body," "my mind," and "my name." As our attachment to these three notions grows stronger and stronger, we become more and more exclusively concerned with our own well-being. All our striving for comfort, our intolerance of life's annoying circumstances, our preoccupation with pleasure and pain, wealth and poverty, fame and obscurity, praise and blame, are due to this idea of "I."

We are usually so obsessed with ourselves that we hardly ever even think about the welfare of others—in fact, we are no more interested in others than a tiger is interested in eating grass. This is completely the opposite of the outlook of the Bodhisattva. The ego is really just a fabrication of thought, and when you realize that both the object grasped and the mind that grasps are void, it is easy to see that others are not different from yourself. All the energy we normally put into looking after ourselves, Bodhisattvas put into looking after others. If a Bodhisattva sees that by plunging into the fires of hell he can help even a single being, he does it without an instant of hesitation, like a swan entering a cool lake.

Khyentse Rinpoche

The Crowned Buddha statue or **Jowo**, *Tibet's most sacred statue. It is of Bengali origin and was brought to Lhasa from China in the seventh century by Princess Wen-Ch'eng, Chinese bride of King Songtsen Gampo. It is housed in the Jokhang, Lhasa's principal temple. During the Cultural Revolution it was removed and abandoned in a warehouse. But, being of massive bronze, it was not destroyed and was later restored to its former place in the Jokhang. The crown of red-colored gold, set with corals and turquoise, was destroyed, but this new one has been offered by the faithful in recent years.*

The seven-story temple building which rises from the uppermost terrace of the Potala, the Dalai Lama's winter quarters in Lhasa.

The eighth-century Tibetan king Trisong Detsen decided to construct a temple on this site. Looking for a priest to consecrate the ground, he consulted Nyang Tingdzin Zangpo, the teacher most venerated by the king. By his insight, Tingdzin Zangpo knew that in Zahor, in Eastern India, lived a great abbot called Shantarakshita. He imparted this information to the king, and the abbot was invited to Tibet. Shantarakshita then tried to consecrate the temple site. But a water-spirit, knowing that the thicket in which he lived was going to be cut down, called all the spirits to his aid, and gathering together in an army, by night the spirits destroyed whatever had been built by men during the day, putting all the earth and stones back where they had come from.

The king went to the abbot and asked for an explanation. "Is it because my obscurations are too dense? Or have you not blessed the site? Must my plans remain unrealized?"

"I have mastered love and compassion," the abbot replied, "but gods and demons cannot be subdued by such peaceful methods. Only wrathful methods will work. At this moment there is in Bodh Gaya, in India, a teacher known as Padmasambhava of Uddiyana. He came into the world in a miraculous way. He has mastered the five sciences and harnessed the power of the absolute. He has attained both the common and supreme accomplishments. He makes all gods and demons tremble, and subjugates the elemental spirits. If you invite him here, no spirit will be able to resist him and all your wishes will be realized."

So the king sent Ba Trisher, Dorje Dudjom, Chim Shakyaprabha and Shübu Palgyi Senge to India, each of them carrying a measure of gold dust and a gold knot of eternity. They explained to the Master that he was needed in Tibet to bless the site of a temple. The Master promised to come. He set off, stopping along the way to bind the twelve *tenma*, the twelve protectresses, the twenty-one *genyen,* and all the gods and spirits of Tibet to firm oaths. Finally he arrived at Trakmar to pacify the site, and the Spontaneously Arisen Temple of Samye was built. It had a three-story central building, surrounded by buildings representing the four continents and the subcontinents. The two *Yaksha* temples, upper and lower, represented the sun and moon. The entire complex was enclosed by a wall surmounted by one hundred and eight stupas. The abbot Shantarakshita, the *acharya* Padmasambhava and the Indian *pandita* Vimalamitra threw flowers for its consecration three times, and many marvelous signs and miracles were seen.

Patrul Rinpoche

Samye Monastery, in the valley of the Tsangpo river in Central Tibet, seen from the hill of Hepori. This photograph was taken during the reconsecration of the temple performed by Khyentse Rinpoche in 1990 (see page 99).

*The newly restored golden roof
of Samye Monastery gleams in the
morning sun.*

Crossing the Brahmaputra river
on the way to Samye Monastery
in a flat-bottomed ferry. The boat
has to cross the wide river in
zigzags to avoid the many sand-
banks. Opposite Khyentse

Rinpoche sits an old monk, holding a vacuum flask, who had
accompanied Khyentse Rinpoche
on his visits to the sick in Lhasa
in the late 1950s before his escape
from Tibet (see page 46).

The valley of Drikung Terdrom,
above Drikung Monastery east of
Lhasa, near the Sun-Rays Cave
where Guru Padmasambhava's

consort and chief disciple, Yeshe
Tsogyal, meditated and realized
the ultimate nature of mind.

The small hermitage at top left encloses the cave of Vairotsana, the first and greatest of all the Tibetan translators (see page 38), in the valley of Nyemo, west of Lhasa. It is said that the depressions in the rock face are the footprints of one hundred thousand dakinis (sky-going female deities).

In the ruins of the massive stone walls of Mindroling Monastery, one of the lamas who accompanied Khyentse Rinpoche to Tibet contemplates the desolation of this erstwhile focus of Buddhist learning and practice, which over many centuries had attracted some of Tibet's finest minds.

At Mindroling Monastery, one of the six main Nyingma monasteries in Tibet, Khyentse Rinpoche meets one of his former friends for the first time in thirty years. The old man is the former retreat master of the famous Kangri Thokar hermitages, where the great fourteenth-century scholar and saint Longchen Rabjam practiced.

At all times, again and again, we should make vast prayers for the sake of all beings. When falling asleep we should think, "May all beings achieve the absolute state"; when waking up, "May all beings awake into the enlightened state"; when getting up, "May all beings obtain the body of a Buddha"; when putting on clothes, "May all beings have modesty and a sense of shame"; when lighting a fire, "May all beings burn the wood of disturbing emotions"; when eating, "May all beings eat the food of concentration"; when opening a door, "May all beings open the door to the city of liberation"; when closing a door, "May all beings close the door to the lower realms"; when going outside, "May I set out on the path to free all beings"; when walking uphill, "May I take all beings to the higher realms"; when walking downhill, "May I go to free beings from the lower realms"; when seeing happiness, "May all beings achieve the happiness of Buddhahood"; when seeing suffering, "May the suffering of all beings be pacified."

Khyentse Rinpoche

At first, you should be driven by a fear of birth and death like a stag escaping from a trap. In the middle, you should have nothing to regret even if you die, like a farmer who has carefully worked his fields. In the end, you should feel relieved and happy, like a person who has just completed a formidable task.

At first, you should know that there is no time to waste, like someone dangerously wounded by an arrow. In the middle, you should meditate on death without thinking of anything else, like a mother whose only child has died. In the end, you should know that there is nothing left to do, like a shepherd whose flocks have been driven off by his enemies.

Gampopa

It is said, "The sign of wisdom is self-control, and the sign of mature spiritual experience is the absence of conflicting emotions." This means that to the same degree that you become wise and learned, you also become serene, peaceful and subdued—not reckless and bursting with pride and arrogance. Year after year, however much your practice progresses, you will be unconcerned about comfort and discomfort, and will have no pride at all. You will always be at peace, untroubled by outer events, with a humble mind, beyond hopes and doubts, and indifferent to the eight worldly concerns—gain and loss, joy and suffering, praise and blame, fame and obscurity. There is a saying that goes: "In spiritual practice, difficulty comes at the beginning, in worldly affairs it comes at the end." This means that, when renouncing ordinary activities and devoting yourself entirely to the practice, you may encounter some outer and inner obstacles; but the more you persevere, the happier you will become.

Conversely, worldly activities bring some ephemeral and superficial satisfaction at first; but eventually they result in bitter disappointment.

Discarding all other thoughts, be concerned only with the inner transformation caused by your practice. Don't be preoccupied by wealth, fame, and power, but cultivate humility—not only for a few months but for your entire life.

Check constantly whether you are succeeding in using the teaching to tame your conflicting emotions. If any practice has the opposite result—increasing your negative emotions and your selfishness—it is not suited to you, and you had better give it up. Once you have started to practice, don't follow just anyone's advice. Be like a wild animal escaping from a trap, who runs as far away as he can. You must get completely free of samsara, not be half in and half out.

When you find yourself in the midst of a large gathering, never lose your mindfulness. Preserve the state of uncontrived simplicity and remember the teacher's instructions.

Be like a mother who has been separated from her newborn baby. A mother is extremely kind and attentive to her baby, and if someone takes the child away from her even for a very short time, she can't stop thinking about him. In the same way, you should never let go of your mindfulness and vigilance.

Even if death were to strike you today like lightning, be ready to die without any sadness or regret, without any residual clinging for what is left behind. Remaining in the recognition of the view, leave this life like an eagle soaring up into the blue sky. When an eagle takes flight into the immensity of the sky, he never thinks, "My wings won't be able to carry me; I won't be able to fly that far." Likewise, when dying, remember your teacher and his instructions, and adhere to them with utter confidence.

Khyentse Rinpoche

The preparations for the cremation of Khyentse Rinpoche in
Bhutan, 1992. Khyentse Rinpoche died in 1991 in Bhutan,
and his body was preserved for
one year to allow disciples from
all over the world to pay their
respects. The cremation took place
in the Paro valley opposite the
"Tiger's Nest," Paro Taktsang (see
page 48) which can be seen in the
distance. Khyentse Rinpoche's
body was cremated in a beautifully decorated stupa, sheltered by
the pagoda-like building on the
left and surrounded by innumerable traditional offerings. In tent
pavilions around the site, the
Bhutanese royal family and guests
and the lamas of different traditions prayed and performed
ceremonies (see page 99). Incense
smoke wafts from the huge crowd
of devotees behind the lower tents.
After the cremation, a permanent
stupa containing Khyentse
Rinpoche's relics was constructed
on the site.

Shechen Rabjam Rinpoche and other lamas stand in their ceremonial dress during *funeral ceremonies for Khyentse Rinpoche held at Shechen Monastery in Nepal.*

A Tibetan woman tends the lamp offerings during funeral ceremonies in Bodhnath, Nepal.

The ultimate teacher, the absolute, is never separate from us,
Yet immature beings, not recognizing this, look outside and seek
　　him far away.
Sole father, with your immense love you have shown me my
　　own wealth;
I, who was a pauper, constantly feel your presence in the depth
　　of my heart.

Wisdom-teacher pervading all the world and beings, samsara
　　and nirvana,
You show how all phenomena can arise as teachings,
Convincing me that everything is the absolute teacher;
I long for ultimate realization, and feel your presence in the
　　depth of my heart.

　　　　　　　　　　　　　　　　　　Khyentse Rinpoche

*The Great Stupa of Bodhnath glows with the light of a hundred
thousand butter-lamps, offered every Friday during the funeral
ceremonies for Khyentse Rinpoche* (see page 99).

LIFE BEYOND TIME

I was in retreat. One day at noon, when the sky was clear, I walked to the summit of the hill above my cave and sat there alone. Toward the north, I saw a pure white cloud billowing over a mountain peak, like milk boiling over. At that moment the memory of my precious spiritual father overwhelmed me, and I sang this song of longing:

To the north, a single great cloud surges over high mountain peaks—
White as overflowing milk.
When I see this, I think of my guru's kindness.

Beneath that distant cloud rise the solitary heights of Auspicious Hermitage.
The way my master once lived in that excellent retreat place
Comes back to my mind.

When I think of his kindness,
Tears well up in my eyes and sorrow in my heart.
My mind is dazed, my perception uncertain—all is hazy and unreal.
How wonderful if he were here again!

I am but an ordinary man, a man with scant devotion.
But still I long to meet him once again.
The master dwells now in absolute space
And his miserable son is left behind in the mire of samsara.

When I see the myriad flowers blooming in the meadows,
I remember the sight of the authentic master.
Then I could see him in person, inspired; now I cannot.
As I think of him over and over again, the master's presence fills my heart.

As I listen to the cuckoo's soft and gentle call,
I remember hearing the authentic master's voice, so deep and sonorous.
Then I could listen to his melodious speech; now I cannot.
As I think of him over and over again, the master's presence fills my heart.

As I see the rising sun spread radiance all around,
I remember the authentic master's wisdom and compassion.
Then he tenderly cared for me; now that time is gone.
As I think of him over and over again, the master's presence fills my heart.

I remember going to see him, having been away for months or years;
The warmth of his welcoming smile comes back to my mind.

No matter in what direction I go, I think of the master;
No matter in what solitary place I stay, I think of the master;
No matter what signs I see, I think of the master—
Always, at all times, I think of my authentic master.

As I sang this plaintive song, the cloud continued to swell until it took the form of a heap of jewels. At the top, in a tent of five-colored rainbow lights, my root guru appeared. Performing a graceful dance, his hands in the gesture of protection, he was more resplendent than ever, peerless in loving kindness. He smiled radiantly and spoke these words in a voice like Brahma's:

Noble son, you who are like my heart,
Do not despair; listen to your father's words.
We, father and son, who came together by the power of past prayers,
    are inseparable
In the state of the luminous absolute nature.

Son, from now on,
Let the length of your practice be the length of your life;
Wander from place to place, in solitary mountain retreats;
By practicing austerities, may you help all fortunate beings.

Don't be sad, look at the mind that feels sadness.
The guru is not other than mind.
It is mind that remembers the guru; it is mind into which the guru dissolves.
Remain in the uncontrived nature of mind, the absolute.

With airy and graceful movements, as though dancing, he rose higher and higher until he vanished like a rainbow into the sky. The clouds too, dissolved into space, and my grief dissolved along with them. I remained for a long while in a serene state beyond thought.

Shabkar

CHANGE AND CONTINUITY, THE SPIRITUAL LEGACY

Transmission and continuity are key points in the Buddhist tradition. The living teachings must not die out; true spiritual realization must be imparted from teacher to disciple. Great Tibetan masters are not isolated mystics. Their wisdom, rooted in the fertile earth of their own confidence and perseverance, has slowly ripened in the sun of their teacher's blessings and wisdom. There are many ways to please one's teacher and repay his kindness, but the way considered best of all is to put his teachings into practice until genuine realization dawns in one's own mind.

Of this way, Khyentse Rinpoche's life was a perfect example. Besides his two main teachers, he studied with more than fifty outstanding masters from all schools of Tibetan Buddhism. Having entirely integrated the teachings into his own being, he could then impart them to thousands of disciples. Among those disciples, a few became true holders of the teachings, his spiritual heirs, and are continuing his lineage today.

Trulshik Rinpoche, born in 1924 (see page 90), is not simply a lineage holder, he is also the principal depositary of Khyentse Rinpoche's "mind treasures," as specifically predicted in the texts of these treasures. He is also the main bestower of monastic vows in the Nyingma lineages and has ordained several thousand monks.

Some thirty years ago, while on pilgrimage in Nepal, Khyentse Rinpoche dreamed one night that he was climbing a lofty mountain. At the summit was a small temple. He entered, and inside he saw, seated side by side, his own former teachers—the three main lamas of Shechen Monastery, Shechen Gyaltsap Rinpoche, Shechen Rabjam, and Shechen Kongtrul. Khyentse Rinpoche prostrated himself before them and, singing in sorrowful verse, asked them how they had suffered in the hands of the Chinese (all three of them having perished in Chinese jails in the late fifties and early sixties). With one voice they replied, also in verse, saying, "For us birth and death are like dreams or illusions. The absolute state knows neither increase nor decline." Khyentse Rinpoche expressed his wish to join them soon in the Buddhafields, since he saw little point in remaining in a world where the teachings were vanishing fast and most teachers were but spurious impostors. At this point, Shechen Kongtrul, gazing at Khyentse Rinpoche with a piercing stare, said, "You must toil to benefit beings and perpetuate the teachings until your last breath. We, the three of us, merging into one, will come

to you as a single incarnation, a helper to fulfill your aims." Soon afterward, in 1966, Khyentse Rinpoche's elder daughter, Chime Wangmo, gave birth to a son whom the sixteenth Karmapa recognized as the incarnation of Shechen Rabjam.

Shechen Rabjam Rinpoche is not only Khyentse Rinpoche's grandson but also his true spiritual heir. He was brought up by his grandfather from the age of five and received every teaching Khyentse Rinpoche gave over twenty-five years. Rabjam Rinpoche says of this extraordinary relationship with his grandfather-teacher:

"My first perception of Khyentse Rinpoche was that of a wonderfully loving grandfather. In fact he was like my true father and mother in one person. Then, as I grew up, this perception gradually transformed into deep respect, confidence, and finally unchanging faith. Khyentse Rinpoche thus became my spiritual master. When I started studying the scriptures, I found in him all the qualities they described for an authentic and realized master. After his death the strength of his presence, far from vanishing, became increasingly all-pervading. I now realize how fortunate I am to have met someone like him. My only aim is to be able to perpetuate his teachings and fulfill his wishes."

This aim Rabjam Rinpoche has been achieving so far with considerable success. From the early age of twenty-five he has had to shoulder the heavy responsibility of looking after the large monasteries of the Shechen tradition in Nepal, Tibet, and Bhutan, as well as that of supervising the construction of another one at Bodh Gaya in India, where the Buddha attained enlightenment.

Khandro Lhamo, Khyentse Rinpoche's wife, at the age of seventy-five in 1987.

Dzongsar Khyentse Rinpoche, born in 1961, is the main incarnation of Khyentse Chökyi Lodrö, Khyentse Rinpoche's other beloved teacher. When the young incarnation was recognized and invited to Sikkim to be enthroned, Khyentse Rinpoche went down to the Sikkim-India border to welcome him. During the few hours' drive back up to Gangtok, Sikkim's capital, Khyentse Rinpoche held the boy on his lap and shed tears all the way. Some other people on that journey later asked him if his apparent sadness was not due to forebodings about the young incarnation's future. But he explained that his tears had been tears of joy and devotion, for during those few hours he had been seeing not the young boy but the former Khyentse Chökyi Lodrö as if in reality. Later, Khyentse Rinpoche used to prostrate himself whenever he met the young incarnation after a long absence—even on a road in the dust. Later, Dzongsar Khyentse Rinpoche became Khyentse Rinpoche's close disciple and received countless teachings and initiations from him. He now heads several monasteries and monastic colleges in India and Bhutan.

It would be futile to name all of Khyentse Rinpoche's disciples, who are, as the Tibetan expression goes, as numerous as stars in an autumn sky. Nevertheless, among the most noteworthy—besides His Holiness the Dalai Lama, of whom we have spoken earlier—are the two Chöling Rinpoches, Namkhai Nyingpo Rinpoche, Jigme Khyentse Rinpoche, Dzigar Kongtrul Rinpoche, Senge Trakpa Rinpoche (an outstanding practitioner who has spent years in solitary retreat), Orgyen Topgyal Rinpoche, and Taklung Tsetrul Pema Wangyal Rinpoche, who is considered by many as the archetype of the ideal disciple and is himself a qualified master. Chogyam Trungpa Rinpoche, Sogyal Rinpoche, and several other disciples of Khyentse Rinpoche have also become influential teachers in the West.

Khyentse Rinpoche's lineage is, therefore, alive and well, and his wisdom and compassion are still warm enough to melt the ore of our being and release the gold of the Buddha-nature within.

Khyentse Rinpoche uncompromisingly lived and breathed the Buddhist teachings. Beyond any particular cultural context, he had the ability to inspire people to question deeply their own choices in life—and then the immense resources of practical experience and wisdom to guide them toward finding their own way. The questions with which the teachings confront us are as fresh and relevant today as ever. Khyentse Rinpoche always insisted that the Buddhist path be treated as something to be lived to the full, an unceasing breath of fresh air, a way to experience things as they truly are.

Khyentse Rinpoche with Rabjam Rinpoche and Pema Wangyal Rinpoche (top left) *and with Dzongsar Khyentse Rinpoche* (below). (top right) *Trulshik Rinpoche* (see text opposite and page 148).

In the beginning I took the teacher as teacher,
In the middle I took the scriptures as teacher,
In the end I took my own mind as teacher.

From the teacher showing the path of deliverance
I received the sacred teachings for my own liberation:
My practice was to shun wrongdoing and cultivate virtue.

From the Bodhisattva teacher
I received the sacred Great Vehicle teachings on how to generate
    enlightened mind:
My practice was to cherish others more than myself.

From the Adamantine Vehicle teacher,
I received the sacred Secret Mantra teachings, empowerments,
    and instructions:
My practice was to cultivate faith, respect, and pure perception.

Shabkar

*Shechen Rabjam Rinpoche wearing the "black hat" costume during a
ceremony at Shechen Monastery. As Khyentse Rinpoche's spiritual heir,
he is now responsible for the Shechen monasteries and their branches
everywhere.*

Shechen Rabjam Rinpoche returned to Tibet to visit Shechen Monastery in 1995. Wherever he went he was greeted with the same magnificent welcome that had been shown to Khyentse Rinpoche on previous occasions. Here, some of Shechen's elder monks keep time with cymbals and drums during the sacred dance festival held in his honor.

The whole thrust of the Buddha's teaching is to master the mind. If you master the mind, you will have mastery over body and speech, and your own and others' suffering can only come to an end. But if you leave the mind full of negative emotions, then however perfect the actions of your body and the words you speak might seem, you are far from the path.

Mastery of the mind is achieved through constant awareness of all your thoughts and actions. Check your mind over and over again, and as soon as negative thoughts arise, remedy them with the appropriate antidotes. When positive thoughts arise, reinforce them by dedicating the merit they bring, wishing that all sentient beings be established in ultimate enlightenment. Maintaining this constant mindfulness in the practices of tranquillity and insight, you will eventually be able to sustain the recognition of wisdom even in the midst of ordinary activities and distractions. Mindfulness is thus the very basis, the cure for all samsaric afflictions.

The practice of Dharma should bring you to the point where you can maintain the same constant awareness whether in or out of practice sessions. This is the quintessential point of all spiritual instruction; without it, however many mantras and prayers you recite, however many thousands of prostrations and circumambulations you do, as long as your mind remains distracted none of it will help to get rid of your obscuring emotions. Never forget this most crucial point.

Khyentse Rinpoche

Their white ceremonial offering scarves at the ready, the monks and lamas of Shechen Monastery hurry toward the monastery's entrance to take part in the welcome celebrations for Shechen Rabjam Rinpoche, after greeting him outside.

THE FULL CIRCLE

As long as space endures,
And as long as sentient beings exist,
May I, too, remain
To dispel the misery of the world.

Shantideva

On December 28, 1995, an unusual number of lamas, monks, and disciples from various parts of the world gathered at Maratika in Eastern Nepal, a place sacred to Guru Padmasambhava. Trulshik Rinpoche, a seventy-two-year-old sage at the head of a colorful procession of monks and devotees, each holding a stick of burning incense, was waiting, gazing at the sky. The crescendo roar of a large Russian helicopter broke the pristine silence of the mountains. Among its twenty-two passengers was the young, newly recognized incarnation of Khyentse Rinpoche.

As the two-and-a-half-year-old child emerged in his mother's arms, Trulshik Rinpoche offered him a long white ceremonial scarf. As if perfectly versed in this traditional greeting, the child placed it intently around Trulshik Rinpoche's neck.

This was no ordinary meeting. Trulshik Rinpoche was the lama who, from the distance of his isolated monastery near Mount Everest, had identified the young boy as the incarnation of his beloved teacher, Dilgo Khyentse Rinpoche.

After Khyentse Rinpoche's death in 1991, his close students had naturally turned to Trulshik Rinpoche, his most senior and accomplished disciple, to find his incarnation.

Since that time, Trulshik Rinpoche had had dreams and visions that clearly indicated the identity of the incarnation. In particular, one vision included a

four-line poem revealing the year of the child's birth, the names of his parents, and the place where he could be found. However, he kept these details secret until April 1995, when he sent a letter to Khyentse Rinpoche's grandson, Shechen Rabjam Rinpoche. Decoded, the poem had revealed that the father was Chöling Rinpoche Mingyur Dewai Dorje (himself the son of Tulku Urgyen Rinpoche, one of Khyentse Rinpoche's closest spiritual friends), and the mother Dechen Paldrön. Their son, born on Guru Padmasambhava's birthday, the tenth day of the fifth month of the Bird Year (June 30, 1993), was, as the verse stated, "unmistakably the incarnation of Paljor" (one of Khyentse Rinpoche's names). The Dalai Lama confirmed that this child was Khyentse Rinpoche's reincarnation.

On December 29, a simple and moving ceremony was held in the cavern of Maratika (see opposite page). For those gathered there, some of whom had walked for days from Kathmandu or Bhutan, the sun had risen from within their hearts into the world at large. Thus was fulfilled the prayer that the Dalai Lama wrote, only days after Khyentse Rinpoche left this world:

The more helpless beings are,
The more it is your true nature to love them.
Therefore, to ripen and liberate all beings in this dark age,
Reveal swiftly the moonlike face of your emanation!

The full circle had been drawn.

Inside the cavern of Maratika in Eastern Nepal, Trulshik Rinpoche, surrounded by other lamas, offers religious robes to Khyentse Rinpoche's Yangsi ("one who has come back into existence"), and gives him a name sent by the Dalai Lama: Urgyen Tendzin Jigme Lhundrup, which means "spontaneous and fearless holder of Padmasambhava's teachings." Butter-lamps on ledges and in crevices in the rock light up the cavern, located in a remote area of the hills, three days' walk from the nearest road. Buddhists believe that Guru Padmasambhava, accompanied by his consort, the Indian princess Mandarava, was blessed here by the Buddha of Boundless Life, Amitayus, and attained a state of enlightenment beyond birth and death. The site is also venerated by Hindu ascetics, who spend nights meditating inside the cavern, their songs blending with the shrill cries of the thousands of bats that live on the high, rocky ceiling.

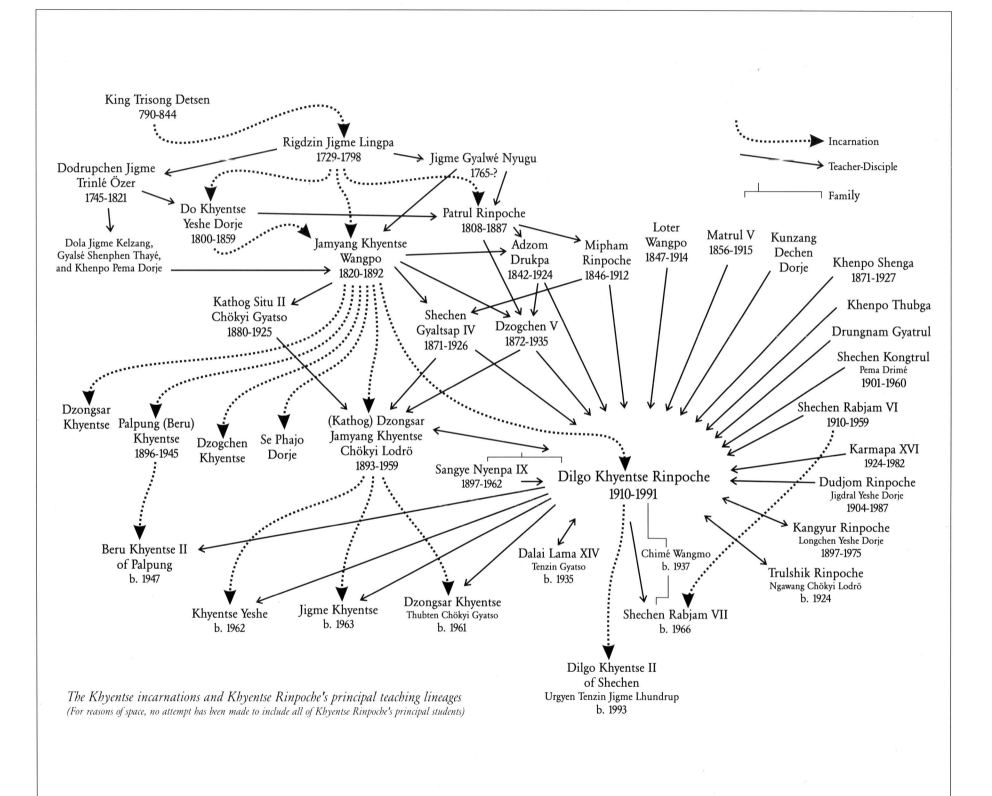

King Trisong Detsen
790-844

Rigdzin Jigme Lingpa
1729-1798

Jigme Gyalwé Nyugu
1765-?

Dodrupchen Jigme
Trinlé Özer
1745-1821

Do Khyentse
Yeshe Dorje
1800-1859

Patrul Rinpoche
1808-1887

Loter
Wangpo
1847-1914

Matrul V
1856-1915

Kunzang
Dechen
Dorje

Dola Jigme Kelzang,
Gyalsé Shenphen Thayé,
and Khenpo Pema Dorje

Jamyang Khyentse
Wangpo
1820-1892

Adzom
Drukpa
1842-1924

Mipham
Rinpoche
1846-1912

Khenpo Shenga
1871-1927

Khenpo Thubga

Kathog Situ II
Chökyi Gyatso
1880-1925

Shechen
Gyaltsap IV
1871-1926

Dzogchen V
1872-1935

Drungnam Gyatrul

Shechen Kongtrul
Pema Drimé
1901-1960

Dzongsar
Khyentse

Palpung (Beru)
Khyentse
1896-1945

Dzogchen
Khyentse

Se Phajo
Dorje

(Kathog) Dzongsar
Jamyang Khyentse
Chökyi Lodrö
1893-1959

Shechen Rabjam VI
1910-1959

Sangye Nyenpa IX
1897-1962

Dilgo Khyentse Rinpoche
1910-1991

Karmapa XVI
1924-1982

Dudjom Rinpoche
Jigdral Yeshe Dorje
1904-1987

Beru Khyentse II
of Palpung
b. 1947

Dalai Lama XIV
Tenzin Gyatso
b. 1935

Chimé Wangmo
b. 1937

Kangyur Rinpoche
Longchen Yeshe Dorje
1897-1975

Trulshik Rinpoche
Ngawang Chökyi Lodrö
b. 1924

Khyentse Yeshe
b. 1962

Jigme Khyentse
b. 1963

Dzongsar Khyentse
Thubten Chökyi Gyatso
b. 1961

Shechen Rabjam VII
b. 1966

Dilgo Khyentse II
of Shechen
Urgyen Tenzin Jigme Lhundrup
b. 1993

Incarnation

Teacher-Disciple

Family

The Khyentse incarnations and Khyentse Rinpoche's principal teaching lineages
(For reasons of space, no attempt has been made to include all of Khyentse Rinpoche's principal students)

This map shows the borders of Tibet
before the communist invasion of 1959.

0	200	500	

Kilometers

POEMS, SONGS, AND TEACHINGS: LIST OF SOURCES

P. 1: Dilgo Khyentse Rinpoche, *Collected Works*, vol. 3; p. 17: Shantideva, *Bodhicaryavatara*; p. 19: Padmasambhava and Chogyur Lingpa, *Lam rim ye shes snying po*; Nagarjuna, *Suhrllekha (bShes spring)*; Chandrakirti; both Shantideva quotes from Shantideva, *Bodhicaryavatara*; Milarepa, *mGur 'bum*; p. 20: Shabkar, *Collected Works*, vol. 1; pp. 26–27: Dilgo Khyentse Rinpoche, *Collected Works*, vol. 23; p. 29: Dilgo Khyentse Rinpoche, *The Heart Treasure of the Enlightened Ones*; Jamgön Kongtrul, *Commentary on Lam rim ye shes snying po*; Shabkar, *Collected Works*, vol. 1; p. 39: Dilgo Khyentse Rinpoche, *Commentary on rGyal sras lag len*; p. 45: Dilgo Khyentse Rinpoche, *Commentary on Ding ri brgya rtsa ma*; pp. 46, 48: all from Dilgo Khyentse Rinpoche, *Collected Works*, vol. 3; p. 49: Maitreya-Asanga, *Uttaratantra-shastra (rGyud bla ma)*; p. 52: Dilgo Khyentse Rinpoche, *The Heart Treasure of the Enlightened Ones*; pp. 54, 57: Shabkar, *Collected Works*, vol. 1; p. 61: Dilgo Khyentse Rinpoche, *Commentary on rGyal sras lag len*; p. 62: Shechen Gyaltsap, *Collected Works*, vol. 5; pp. 66, 67: Shantideva, *Bodhicaryavatara*; p. 72: Dilgo Khyentse Rinpoche, *The Heart Treasure of the Enlightened Ones*; p. 82: Dilgo Khyentse Rinpoche; p. 86: Dilgo Khyentse Rinpoche, *Collected Works*, vol. 3; Dilgo Khyentse Rinpoche, *Commentary on Mipham Rinpoche's Jampel Dzogpachenpo*; pp. 91, 92: both from Shabkar, *Collected Works*, vol. 1; p. 94: Shabkar, *Collected Works*, vol. 1; Shantideva, *Bodhicaryavatara*; p. 96: Shabkar, *Collected Works*, vol. 1; p. 101: Dilgo Khyentse Rinpoche, *Collected Works*, vol. 3; p. 104: Dilgo Khyentse Rinpoche, *The Heart Treasure of the Enlightened Ones*; p. 108: Dilgo Khyentse Rinpoche, *Explanation of Shechen Gyaltsap's commentary on Zurchungpa's Zhal gdams brgyad cu pa, Collected Works of Shechen Gyaltsap*, vol. 5; pp. 113, 117: Shabkar, *Collected Works*, vol. 1; p. 118: Dilgo Khyentse Rinpoche, *The Wish-Fulfilling Jewel*; Jamgön Kongtrul, *Commentary on Lam rim ye shes snying po*; Drikung Kyobpa; *Precious Embodiment Tantra (Kun 'dus rin po che 'i rgyud)*; p. 122: Shabkar, *Collected Works*, vol. 3; p. 124: Buddha Shakyamuni; Dilgo Khyentse Rinpoche, *The Heart Treasure of the Enlightened Ones*; p. 126: Patrul Rinpoche, *The Words of My Perfect Teacher*; p. 133: Dilgo Khyentse Rinpoche, *The Wish-Fulfilling Jewel*; p. 134: Gampopa; Dilgo Khyentse Rinpoche, *Commentary on Jigme Lingpa's Ri chos*; p. 138: Dilgo Khyentse Rinpoche, *Collected Works*, vol. 3; pp. 140–141, 144: both from Shabkar, *Collected Works*, vol. 1; p. 146: Dilgo Khyentse Rinpoche, *The Heart Treasure of the Enlightened Ones*; p. 148: Shantideva, *Bodhicaryavatara*.

Quotations and extracts from the following books have been included by permission of the publishers:

Dilgo Khyentse Rinpoche, *The Wish-Fulfilling Jewel*. Copyright © 1988 by H. H. Dilgo Khyentse Rinpoche. Translated by Padmakara Translation Group. Reprinted by arrangement with Shambhala Publications, Inc., Boston.

Dilgo Khyentse Rinpoche, *The Heart Treasure of the Enlightened Ones*. Copyright © 1992 by H. H. Dilgo Khyentse Rinpoche. Translated by Padmakara Translation Group. Reprinted by arrangement with Shambhala Publications, Inc., Boston.

Patrul Rinpoche, *The Words of My Perfect Teacher*. Copyright © 1994 by Padmakara Translation Group. San Francisco: International Sacred Literature Trust–HarperCollins, 1994 (pages 19, 118, 124, 126, 134).

Shabkar Tsogdruk Rangdrol, *The Life of Shabkar, The Autobiography of a Tibetan Yogin*. Translated by Matthieu Ricard. Copyright © 1994 SUNY Press, Albany, New York.

Padmasambhava and Jamgon Kongtrul the Great, *The Light of Wisdom*. Copyright © 1995 by Erik Hein Schmidt. Reprinted by arrangement with Shambhala Publications, Inc., Boston.

Shantideva, *The Way of the Bodhisattva (Bodhicaryavatara)*. Copyright © 1996 by Padmakara Translation Group. Reprinted by arrangement with Shambhala Publications, Inc., Boston.

Other books by Dilgo Khyentse Rinpoche published in English translation:

Enlightened Courage. Translated by Padmakara Translation Group. Peyzac-le-Moustier, France: Éditions Padmakara, 1992 and Ithaca, New York: Snow Lion, 1994.

The Excellent Path to Enlightenment. Translated by Padmakara Translation Group. Kathmandu: Shechen Tennyi Dargyeling, 1987. Second edition, Ithaca, New York: Snow Lion, forthcoming.

Readers interested in the activities of Shechen Foundation, which is dedicated to the preservation of Tibetan Buddhist philosophy and culture, may contact Shechen Foundation, 36 West 20th Street, New York, NY 10011. Fax (718) 846-3751.

The photographs in this book were taken with Nikon FM2 cameras on Kodachrome 64, Fuji Velvia 50, and Fuji Provia 100 films.

The Padmakara Translation Group is located at Laugeral, 24290 Saint-Léon-sur-Vézère, France.

Copyright © 2000 by Aperture Foundation, Inc. Photographs copyright © 2000 by Matthieu Ricard Text copyright © 2000 by Padmakara Translation Group Remembrance copyright © 2000 His Holiness the Dali Lama Excerpts from the writing of Dilgo Khyentse Rinpoche copyright © 2000 Shechen Foundation. Photograph on page 9 copyright © 2000 Christian Bruyat, reprinted with permission.

The Spirit of Tibet was originally published in 1996 by Aperture as *Journey to Enlightenment*.

Library of Congress Catalog Card Number: 00-108633
Paperback ISBN: 0-89381-903-4
Hardcover ISBN: 0-89381-956-5
Printed by Sing Cheong Printing Co., Ltd., Hong Kong

Book design and typesetting by Wendy Byrne
Cover design by Olga Gourko

The Staff at Aperture for *The Spirit of Tibet* is:
Michael E. Hoffman, Executive Director;
Michael Lorenzini, Project Manager/Assistant Editor;
Melissa Harris, Senior Editor; Diana Stoll, Associate Editor;
Stevan A. Baron, V.P., Production;
Helen Marra, Production Manager;
Lesley A. Martin, Editorial Work-Scholar;
Meredith Hinshaw, Production Work-Scholar

Aperture Foundation publishes a periodical, books, and portfolios of fine photography and presents world-class exhibitions to communicate with serious photographers and creative people everywhere. A complete catalog is available upon request. Aperture Customer Service: 20 East 23rd Street, New York, New York 10010. Phone: (212) 598-4205. Fax: (212) 598-4015. Toll-free: (800) 929-2323. E-mail: customerservice@aperture.org Aperture Foundation, including Book Center and Burden Gallery: 20 East 23rd Street, New York, New York 10010. Phone: (212) 505-5555, ext. 300. Fax: (212) 979-7759. E-mail: info@aperture.org Visit Aperture's website: www.aperture.org

10 9 8 7 6 5 4 3 2 1